If You Love This Country

■■■■■■■■■■■■■■■■■■■■■■■■■■■■■■■

If You Love This Country:

Facts and Feelings on

Free Trade

assembled by
Laurier LaPierre

Canadian Cataloguing in Publication Data

Main entry under title:
If you love this country: facts and feelings on free trade

ISBN 0-7710-4697-9

1. Free trade and protection – Protection.   2. Canada –
Commercial policy.   3. Canada – Commerce – United States.
4. United States – Commerce – Canada.
I. LaPierre, Laurier L., 1929 – .

.HF1766.I44 1987   382.7'0971   C88-093034-9

Cover and book design by Robert Burns, Burns & Company

Printed and bound in Canada

McClelland and Stewart
The Canadian Publishers
481 University Avenue
Toronto, Ontario
M5G 2E9

■■■■■■■■■■■■■■■■■■■■■■■■■■■■■■■

I have sat by night beside a cold lake
And touched things smoother than moonlight on still water

from ''Trans Canada'' by F.R. Scott

Contents

What We Feel . . .

Foreword from the Publisher

This book is an urgent contribution to the public debate on the critical issue of the Canada-U.S. Free Trade Agreement and the underlying assumptions it poses for the future of Canada. All the contributors helped to put this book together with unprecedented rapidity in the past few weeks because they wanted all Canadians to know what they know, feel what they feel. The emotion is part of what we know with our minds and feel with our hearts – that Canadians must have a chance to decide what our country must be.

Adrienne Clarkson

Free Trade

The United States of

America

Forget this!
Peter Murphy.

No.
David Peterson.

Very funny!
Simon.

...continue... will...

HA! HA! U.S. CONGRESS.

shake

down

This world harm the Italian designers Mila!

Canada

And kill my T.V. series? Shelly.

forever.

"Mais ululwoorey.."
"Ronald Reagan

AISLIN '87.
MONTREAL
GAZETTE

Introduction

Dear Reader:

We the people who have contributed to this book want to tell you how dangerous the Canada-U.S. Free Trade Agreement is to the survival of our country as we experience it day by day.

All of us travelled a long journey to where we are now. In the process we have learned to embrace the future. We want to have one *in* Canada for ourselves and for our children.

To welcome change: we fight outdated concepts; we chart new courses; and we bear the scars of involvement. Canada has nourished and sustained us. We want to preserve it.

En tant qu'écrivains et artistes, syndicalistes et administrateurs, enseignants, économistes et journalistes, nous avons le devoir et le droit de participer à ce débat qui déterminera l'avenir de notre pays. Nous sommes aussi convaincus que cet accord n'est que le premier

13

■■■■■■■■■■■■■■■■■■■■■■■■■■■■■■■■

d'une série qui finira par détruire le Canada. Nous voulons vous en prévenir.

For a living we develop concepts and explore ideas. So we pay close attention to the written and spoken word. On the evidence of the documents made public by the governments of Canada and the United States on the free trade agreement, we may categorically state that what our negotiators and leaders led us to believe is not what they initialled at the beginning of October, 1987. The thousand pages of the final text (to be delivered only God knows when) will not change that.

What follows in these pages is a *cri de coeur* imploring you to recognize the debate over the Canada-U.S. Free Trade Agreement as the most important moment in our national life. It is not possible for you, any more than for us, to stand idly by as Canada becomes engulfed in the American manifest destiny.

If you love this country . . . you will hear us out.

If you love this country . . . you will choose Canada.

Sincerely yours,
Laurier LaPierre
Britannia Beach, British Columbia
Canada

PS: Adrienne Clarkson brought us together; Marty Katz and Jim Oakes kept track of us; and Joyce Wayne and the good people at McClelland and Stewart made it happen. I thank them.

What We Think**·················**

(if)

■■■■■■■■■■■■■■■■■■■■■■■■■■■■■

"... the only position they've ever adopted toward us, country to country, has been the missionary position ..."

Margaret Atwood

Margaret Atwood grew up in northern Quebec and has lived in Vancouver, Edmonton, Montreal, and rural Ontario. A writer of international prominence, she is well known in the U.S., Europe, and Australia. She is a former president of the Writers Union of Canada and a Governor General's Award winner for poetry and fiction.

I believe this issue has the potential to fragment and destroy the country in a way that nothing else has succeeded in doing. I would dearly like to hope that this agreement is going to be in some way "good for the country." Why? Partly because it's Canadian to take that attitude: as a nation, we do tend to have this touching and naive belief that those in authority know what they're doing. But also because, if someone comes along and puts a hand over your eyes and shoves an unknown, dubious substance down your throat, all you've got to fall back on is hope. You just hope like heck that it's going to turn

■■■■■■■■■■■■■■■■■■■■■■■■■■■■■■■■■

out to be good for you in the end. But hope is no substitute for reality.

So I'm sitting around reading the rhetoric in the newspapers, with my ears aflap for news, open to being convinced. But so far I'm not, and I'd like to share with you some of the reasons why not, and put to you some of the questions that trouble my waking hours, and even my sleeping ones, during which Dief the Chief appears to me in dreams, jowls quivering in outrage, and asks me what's going on and why the Prime Minister began by saying that free trade would threaten Canada's sovereignty but changed his mind after the election, while Sir John A. Macdonald revolves rapidly in his grave. ''Don't ask me, ask them,'' I say. But ghosts have a way of visiting only those who remember them.

My first worry is that there are no hard facts. Why not? For the simple reason that nobody can predict the future. No matter how many graphs you draw up, as long as they are graphs about the future they don't necessarily hold any more water than a leaky boot. The future is like life after death. You can say anything you like about it, because nobody can actually go there and come back and tell us about it. We know more or less what we're giving up – though we won't know the whole of it till after the small print has been passed through the mental digestive systems of the lawyers – but we can't know what we're getting in return. In short, I don't understand the full scope and implications of this agreement and I don't believe anyone else really does either. Maybe I'm just stupid, but if so there's a lot more stupid people like me running around loose.

But there are two things in particular, having to do with the cultural community, that appear to have been sacrificed so far. These things do not affect me financially in any large way but I must say what I think their effects will be. One is the film distribution policy, which will soon appear, we are given to understand, in a very watered-down form, because the original would have displeased the great star-spangled Them and interfered with this agreement. There goes the Canadian film industry in any major form. I would love to stand corrected on this. The other is the abolition of special postal rates for Canadian magazines. There go our national magazines, not to mention our literary magazines – which, as any writer who has come up through the ranks will tell you, are the only entry to the larger literary marketplace for most young writers. Unless steps are taken to counterbalance the effects of this, we're going to be way worse off on the magazine front than we were even in 1960. This deal also severely limits our power to introduce any *new* initiatives on the cultural front. It gives us, not more freedom of movement, but much less.

Second point: We're told that polls show a 49 per cent in-favour response, but I distrust polls. Why? Because I have a background in market research, and I know that the answers you get depend a lot on how you ask the questions. I expect that, if the poll question is simply "Are you in favour of free trade?" you're going to get a certain amount of *Yes* because "free" is a positive word, as in free gift, free lunch, free world, and free speech. But if you asked, "Are you in favour of this particular trade deal if it means you have to give up your health insurance, unemployment benefits, and regional development aid – which remain vulnerable to challenge as unfair subsidies under U.S. trade law – and if you also have to give up Canada's foreign affairs autonomy and our visibility in arts and entertainment – and if it means the loss of a million jobs, with only vague notions of how they'll be replaced – and if it also means we're committed to playing only by the other guy's rules?" I expect you'd get a different response. And what if you asked, "Are you in favour of this deal if it means the disintegration of Canada?" Maybe that's something we *should* ask. In other words, do we really want a country? A level playing field, after all, is one from which all distinguishing features have been removed. One category of job that's not

■■■■■■■■■■■■■■■■■■■■■■■■■■■■■■■■

on the table in this deal is that of federal Member of Parliament. But if that august body is divesting itself of its powers, the ordinary taxpayer is going to start asking, sooner or later, what's Ottawa for? What powers remain? I mean, why pay extra? If it's Washington making the decisions anyway, why deal with the middleman? Why don't we just join them? Canada as a separate but dominated country has done about as well under the U.S. as women, worldwide, have done under men; about the only position they've ever adopted toward us, country to country, has been the missionary position, and we were not on the top. I guess that's why the national wisdom vis-à-vis Them has so often taken the form of lying still, keeping your mouth shut, and pretending you like it. But as part of *Them*, at least we'd get to vote, eh? We'd sure as heck fit in; we already know more about them than we know about one another, or so you'd think. Short form: Can Canada? If Canada can't, can it.

Third point: It's no use ridiculing scenarios like this, or calling people who talk about them cowards or idiots or Nazis or self-interested, all of which terms have been bandied about recently, just as it's no good calling pro-free-traders cowards or idiots or Nazis or self-interested. It's no good accusing people of wrapping themselves in the flag, and I might point out in passing that it seems to be okay in the States to do this flag-wrapping act – they have this thing called patriotism, it's thought of as standing up for yourself – but in Canada it's seen as bad taste or even subversive. I wonder why.

May I suggest that instead of name-calling, each side should try to find out what will *really* be "good" for the country. This throws us back to Philosophy 101: how do you define "good"? Is it only money we're talking about here? I don't think so. Canadian people, like people everywhere, have values other than money that are important to them. Their fears of losing these values are real fears, by which I mean that they are truly held and must be addressed. It's no use claiming that there is some

■■■■■■■■■■■■■■■■■■■■■■■■■■■■■■■■■

mysterious gene of Canadianness, welded into us at conception, that will guarantee the retention of these values even if all the social structures, educational underpinnings, and cultural manifestations of them disappear. What will be done, if anything, to give these values a fighting chance of surviving? As George Bernard Shaw commented when a beautiful actress wanted to have a child with him so it would have her looks and his brains, "But madam – what if it has *my* looks and *your* brains?" We'd like to think we're about to get the best of both worlds – Canadian stability and a more caring society, plus American markets – but what if instead we get their crime rate, health programs, and gun laws, and they get our markets, or what's left of them?

It's no use saying that this is mere anti-Yank paranoia; a lot of us get on just fine in the country of superlatives, and as for myself it's the land of my ancestors and the haunt of my youth. It's not about liking the great Them, it's about wanting to be who you are. Anyone from Quebec understands the connections among culture, society, and politics, although others sometimes have to have it spelled out. Short form: just because you like women doesn't mean you want to be one.

And it's no use saying that these are emotional arguments, as if that disqualifies them. Almost all of the arguments heard so far in this debate have been emotional arguments. Fear is an emotion, yes, and love of country is an emotion; but greed is an emotion, too.

Some questions us voters would like answered

1. Has the government signed away its flexibility? The world is in for a rocky ride over the next few years, and shifts in economic ground will demand well-honed and very quick responses. Right now, Wall Street has turned tail and is demanding interventionist fiscal policies it would have spat on even a few months ago. How much room for manoeuvring are we leaving ourselves?

2. Along those lines – if you're going to hitch your

21

■■■■■■■■■■■■■■■■■■■■■■■■■■■■■■■■

wagon to a star – if you're going to merge your economy totally with another one – why not a rising star instead of one that's hovering so close to burnout? How about those U.S. budget and trade deficits? (You're looking at someone who agrees with the Wilsonian goal of reducing the deficit.) Why not a free trade deal with Japan, which, once it connects with the huge markets in India and China and Southeast Asia, is going to eclipse the U.S? Do we really want to risk going down with the *Titanic?* Have we explored viable alternatives? Have we even removed barriers to trade among the provinces? Biologically speaking, the animals that survive in tough times are generalists, not specialists. They keep their range of options wide. Are we doing that?

3. A related question: Do we have a fall-back position? What if we do this and it turns into a mess? Can we get out of it?

4. The U.S. is already our major trading partner, and vice versa. Why are we sacrificing our options as a society over a "comprehensive" trade deal that is really about the small percentage left?

5. Fifth and most important point: *Why are we doing this so fast?* This committee doesn't even have a text of the final agreement. As a writer I would never sign a contract under those conditions. This is a major structural change, and nobody's being given a chance to really look at it. Nor is it the U.S. timetable that's forcing the bulldoze act, apparently: it's our side that's in such an all-fired rush. The final text appears, we have a few days to examine it, and bingo! As one businessman said to me privately, "It's not a very good deal, but it's the only deal around so we should grab it." This is an old snake-oil salesman technique – get some now because there's only one left. Is this last-day sale mentality the right approach to deciding the future of a people? Is it even democratic?

We need more time, to see a lot more exactly who may be affected and in what ways. We need an INFORMED, TRUTHFUL, NATIONAL debate. We need an election.

■■■■■■■■■■■■■■■■■■■■■■■■■■■■■■

Our national animal is the beaver, noted for its industry and its co-operative spirit. In medieval bestiaries it is also noted for its habit, when frightened, of biting off its own testicles and offering them to its pursuer. I hope we are not succumbing to some form of that impulse.

■■■■■■■■■■■■■■■■■■■■■■■■■■■

"For the first time, Canadians have had to ask themselves what kind of people we are and what kind of people we want to be."

Pierre Berton

Pierre Francis de Marigny Berton was born in Dawson City, Yukon. He has been a journalist since 1942 and is one of Canada's most cherished writers. Mr. Berton makes his home in Kleinburg, Ontario.

The free trade issue goes to the very heart of our national character. Americans don't really understand how different we are. Their leadership doesn't understand it, nor does Mr. Murphy. What distresses me is the realization that our own government doesn't appear to understand it either. The suspicion persists that Mr. Mulroney, who rose to prominence as the chief executive officer of an American-owned company, is quite prepared to bargain away some of those very aspects of our society that *make* us distinctive.

It is traditionally the Liberals and not the Tories who have cosied up to the Yanks. They were the continental-

■■■■■■■■■■■■■■■■■■■■■■■■■■■■■■■■

ists; the Conservatives, the Chinese wall protectionists. After all, our first Prime Minister, John A. Macdonald, was able to roar back into office after the greatest political scandal of the century on the strength of his "National Policy." Macdonald, the high-tariff Tory, launched and then propped up the tottering Canadian Pacific Railway to prevent the American expansionists from grabbing the Canadian West. No free trade for him.

See him now, on that memorable December day in 1880. He is old and tired, his face veined from too much gin and too much port, but pale now from a crippling stomach ailment that makes it all but impossible for him to stand. Yet stand he does for more than three hours, delivering the finest speech of his career, hammering home the adverbs as he cries out that the railway will be built, "vigorously, continuously, systematically and successfully!" It will be an all-Canadian line "which will give us a great and united, rich and improving, developing Canada, instead of making us tributary to American bondage, to American tolls, to American freights, to all the little tricks and big tricks that the American railways are addicted to for the purpose of destroying our road." This is vintage Macdonald, the bold rhetoric that turned him into a Canadian icon.

When Mulroney, flushed with a massive electoral victory, made free trade the main thrust of his new government, the country responded with enthusiasm. *Wow*! More jobs! Lower prices on imported American goods! Cheaper TV sets, stereos, wine, shoes, even automobiles! No more lining up at customs counters; no more shabby attempts at smuggling; no more petty irritations from petty officials! It sounded too good to be true and it was.

In the past couple of years, support for free trade in Canada has been eroded steadily as Canadians come to grips with the realities of Mulroney's grand design. Today, close to half the population is opposed or lukewarm. For when the chips are down, we Canadians have always been willing to pay a price for living in this small, peaceable kingdom. And the price is beginning to look pretty high.

Subsidy. That's a great Canadian word, but it's anathema to American businesses that want to compete in Canada. In this country we subsidize everything from Atlantic fishermen to prairie farmers, from book publishers to aircraft companies. The shape and nature of the country demand that the strong prop up the weak. That philosophy is so deeply ingrained in the Canadian tradition that it's unthinkable to abandon it. Under free trade the social, cultural, and economic net that we have so laboriously woven to protect our identity simply boils down to unfair trade practices. Unemployment insurance? Medicare? Family allowances? These are subsidies that allow Canadians to compete unfairly in the wage and salary market.

As for culture – Canadians and Americans don't even speak the same language. They think of culture in terms of opera, ballet, and classical music. To us it covers everything from Stompin' Tom Connors to *Hockey Night in Canada*. What is merely "industry" to them is culture to us. Books, movies, radio, television – all culture. Anne Murray is culture. Wayne and Shuster are culture. *Maclean's* magazine is culture. Farley Mowat is culture. The government subsidizes them all, in one way or another, because all are genuine Canadian artefacts, distinct and unique, something we have that nobody else has – the ingredients of our national mucilage.

Why should Canadian radio stations be forced to play so much Canadian music? Why should Canadian advertisers be penalized if they want to use American border television stations? What's all this nonsense about film quotas? Why can't *Time* magazine publish a Canadian edition without the government setting out the rules? To Canadians this is a necessary form of cultural protectionism; to those who think of Canada as another state in the union – part of the American domestic market – it's unfair competition.

■■■■■■■■■■■■■■■■■■■■■■■■■■■■■■■■■

Not long ago, the American ambassador to Canada, discussing this question of cultural sovereignty, made a remark about television so appalling in its ignorance that one wondered what flat stone he'd been languishing under. He said he couldn't understand why Canadians were so steamed up about the predominance of American programs on our networks. Why, said he, PBS network in the U.S. was loaded with British imports but his countrymen weren't a bit concerned about this threat to their sovereignty! This remark went unchallenged in Canada, probably because the idea of American culture being threatened by *Masterpiece Theatre* was so ludicrous that it didn't require comment. But if a leading diplomat is so myopic, what hope could our negotiating team have had in Washington?

Americans and Canadians are two different peoples: we run our country in a different fashion than the Americans do, not necessarily better and not necessarily worse, but in our own way – a way that happens to fit our peculiar environmental, cultural, economic, and historic background. Can we hang on to this Canadian way and still enjoy the advantages of free trade? That's what the discussion is all about.

At the turn of the century we got the short end of the stick in negotiations over the Alaska boundary. As a result we've been denied a saltwater port on the part of British Columbia that is blocked by the Alaska panhandle. In 1947, a group of Hollywood sharpies came up to Ottawa and convinced the Canadian government to scrap its plans for a film quota. Ever since then almost every nickel made at a Canadian box office by an American movie has gone back to the United States. Had the government insisted that some of it be invested here we might now have a thriving film industry. And then in the 1950s, in spite of the valiant efforts of Andy McNaughton, we handed over Columbia River power on a platter. British Columbia has been trying to get it back ever since. In the light of these past follies it's hard to see how we could have come out

27

■■■■■■■■■■■■■■■■■■■■■■■■■■■■■■

of the current discussions without surrendering some of those peculiar institutions and practices that help make us a distinct and sovereign people. Not everybody in Canada worries about this; but it's this fear that's at the basis of the free trade debate.

And that, of course, is the kicker. In the end the discussion about free trade may be seen as more important than free trade itself. All unwittingly, Mr. Mulroney has plunged this country into a full-scale debate about the nature of Canada and its institutions. For the first time, Canadians have had to ask themselves what kind of people we are and what kind of people we want to be. How important is this network of support we've fashioned for ourselves? What parts of it are we prepared to give up? What will we insist on keeping no matter what the cost? The marathon argument over reciprocity, which some have seen as divisive, has actually drawn us together as a people. It's been a learning experience for everybody: for the pundits and the labour leaders, for the businessmen and the blue-collar workers, for the scribblers and the politicians.

It's also been a learning experience, I suggest, for the Right Honourable Brian Mulroney.

"... the more it hurts, the brighter your smile."

Matt Cohen

Matt Cohen is a novelist of great sophistication and originality, whose latest novel is Nadine. *Much of his writing has been inspired by the country north of Kingston, where he has a farm.*

Six Reasons Why I Cannot Contribute To This Volume
One: According to Canada's chief trade negotiator people who oppose the Mulroney deal with the United States are behaving "like Nazis." Being called names by the government is too scary.

Two: The government has explained that it is protecting culture in the new agreement. As yet unreleased text contains strict provisions for this. Included is a clause that states categorically that if in the opinion of a binational tribunal Canadian culture *does* appear to be suffering because of the agreement, there will be a cross-country egg-painting contest with trips to Holly-

▪▪▪▪▪▪▪▪▪▪▪▪▪▪▪▪▪▪▪▪▪▪▪▪▪▪▪▪▪▪

wood for the winners. I don't want to jeopardize my chances.

Three: (Perhaps) unlike most contributors to this volume I have always considered some form of "economic union" with the U.S. or North American continentalism to be inevitable. I thought, in my now – I realize – mistaken way, that this "union" would be subtly or otherwise forced upon us by our more powerful neighbour. But what is being proposed now has been initiated not by them but by us. Does this mean that some of them are pretending to be us? Or have we, unbeknownst to ourselves, become them? One possible conclusion is that we are not us and they are not them, in which case, whether or not I am me, I don't know whose side I'm on. The other possible conclusion is we are obliterating ourselves for no reason. On the other hand, if we do obliterate ourselves, we no longer have to worry about them becoming us.

Four: A Toronto intellectual I know, a man who has deep thoughts while reading *The New York Times* and sipping cappucino, told me that free trade would make Canadians richer because "economic theory" says that free trade makes people richer. He also told me that I shouldn't worry about free trade because the deal we are presented with – or, at least, are going to be presented with – is not really free trade but an exemption from certain American laws that might be passed in years to come. Although we don't know what these laws are because they don't yet exist, our crafty and brilliant government has protected us by giving away a bunch of stuff that already does exist. "The deal," he explained to me, "is like going to the dentist: *the more it hurts, the brighter your smile*."

Five: If I write about "the deal" then ten or twenty or thirty years from now my children or their children might find this book at the bottom of some pile. Imagine having to explain the concept of "Canada" a generation from now. Imagine having to explain that in one apparently

■■■■■■■■■■■■■■■■■■■■■■■■■■■■■■

innocent year we first established a "national" constitution by taking away the rights of women, native peoples, and northerners, then solidified our economy by deciding to run it according to the rules of another country.

Six: After learning in public school how to sing "God Save the Queen," name the forty-eight states, and say the Lord's Prayer, I was taught that if you can't say something nice, you shouldn't say anything at all.

■■■■■■■■■■■■■■■■■■■■■■■■■■■■■■■■■■■

"The issues are not simply a matter of economics."

The Right Reverend Remi De Roo

Bishop Remi De Roo, the Roman Catholic Bishop of Victoria, is a passionate defender of the poor, native peoples, and the disenfranchised of South and Central America. He is best noted for his 1983 New Year's statement entitled "Ethical Reflections on the Economic Crisis," issued by the Social Affairs Commission of Canada's Catholic bishops.

As this historic debate heats up across the country, I hear numerous voices of concerned people. They fear they will be the victims of the economic restructuring that would result from a U.S.-Canada free trade accord. These voices include many people: workers in manufacturing industries; working women in service industries; people on social assistance and fixed incomes; farmers and fishers in certain sectors; artists, writers, and entertainers in cultural enterprises; native peoples and other marginalized groups in Canada's economy and society. As a pastor, I share their fears, anxieties, and concerns about the proposed free trade pact. As a citizen and a theologian, I discern that the pact has profound ethical significance and presents us with a number of moral issues.

One of my preoccupations is that the public debate has so far been mainly concerned with the internal impacts of free trade on our society. This focus on the negative impact of free trade on Canadian social policies, national priorities, and cultural distinctiveness is important. But it is also urgent that we place ourselves outside of the North American perspective to see what external impacts a U.S.-Canada accord will have on peoples elsewhere in the world. Today we are part of a global family. I am particularly concerned with the potential impact on Canada's responsibilities toward the poor and oppressed peoples in what we call the Third World.

From a global perspective, the proposed U.S.-Canada trade accord looks like a major step toward the building of fortress North America. In a highly competitive global economic climate, a comprehensive free trade pact would constitute a new form of continental protectionism. Experience shows that closer economic ties have generated closer political bonds between Canada and the U.S. Canadian complicity in the war in Vietnam, the questioning of Canada's neutrality occasioned by the cruise missile tests, the militarization of the economy through defence production sharing, and our ambivalent attitude toward Central America all reflect this in one way or another. As a result, serious questions must be raised about the further impact of this accord on Canada's capacity to act as a sovereign national state with an independent foreign policy.

Increasingly, various international justice and peace organizations in Canada are identifying some critical implications of a comprehensive free trade accord. For example:

1. Those Third World countries seeking enhanced trade relations with Canada will likely face much

■■■■■■■■■■■■■■■■■■■■■■■■■■■■■■

more intense competition for Canadian markets due to the preferential treatment that will be accorded U.S. products in Canada. What will this do to Canada's ability to develop mutual trade relations with those Third World countries struggling to reorganize their economies to serve the basic needs of their peoples?

2. Canada could well face further restrictions on its capacity to promote human rights in certain repressive regimes, especially those countries or regions that come under American economic or military spheres of influence. It is not too fanciful to ask whether Canada would be called upon to support U.S. policies backing the Contras in Nicaragua.

3. Canada's refugee and immigration policies are likely to become even more restrictive, favouring wealthy entrepreneurs required for a high-tech market economy rather than people struggling to escape from conditions of poverty and political repression. Is this not already apparent in the so-called "emergency" refugee legislation (Bills C-55 and C-84) recently rammed through Parliament?

4. Canada's responsibilities in promoting nuclear disarmament could also be further constrained by the increased involvement of Canadian industries in arms production that would probably result from closer ties to the U.S. military economy. Will this mean greater pressure on Canada to support the U.S. Star Wars program, further cruise missile tests, and develop a nuclear submarine fleet in the Arctic?

Closer economic ties with the United States through the proposed free trade accord would increase the potential for economic retaliation by our neighbour to the south. Under the proposed agreement, Canada would remain subject to the exercise of U.S. countervail duties and other U.S. trade remedy laws. These economic realities, in turn, would likely heighten Canada's difficulties in pursuing a more independent foreign policy in the closing decade of this twentieth century.

Twenty years ago, Pope Paul VI warned in his encyclical ''On the Development of Peoples'' that ''the rule of free trade, taken by itself, should no longer govern international relations.'' The reasons, he argued, had to do with the gross inequalities of global market systems. Under these conditions, the basic development needs of smaller nations are dominated by the interests of larger, more powerful nation-states and transnational corporations.

When judging free trade we should take into account the survival-of-the-fittest mentality presently dominating international economic relations. The shock waves that reverberated around the globe with the wild fluctuations of the stock markets were very revealing. *The ruthless competition which is today the supreme law of economics appears to me as morally unacceptable*. To achieve lasting global peace based on justice we need a co-operative global economy based on mutually interdependent market systems. Fortress North America is not the answer. The issues are not simply a matter of economics. Global humanism is involved here.

It is certainly true that the world has become highly competitive. We cannot escape that fact. But we still have time to consider alternatives, and our very survival as an independent economic partner in a future collaborative global economy may be at stake. The fundamental ethical choices and political challenges are clear. We are more than adequately involved with the United States already. What we need to promote now is a self-reliant Canadian economy, meeting the basic needs of all our people, coupled with more diversified and collaborative trade relations with the peoples of the Third World countries. From a humanitarian and ethical perspective, we Canadians owe this contribution to ourselves and to the world.

36

«Nous dépêtrer du déclin de l'empire américain ou nous y enliser».

Andrée Ferretti

Andrée Ferretti est une activiste qui a joué un rôle important dans les mouvements syndicaux et indépendantistes du Québec. Elle vient de publier Renaissance en Paganie. *Elle demeure à Montréal.*

Il est symptomatique de la crise que nous vivons – crise des idées autant que crise du système — que le débat amorcé autour d'un éventuel accord de libre-échange entre le Canada et les États-Unis, ne déborde quasiment pas l'analyse économiste, simpliste s'il en est une, car incapable de remettre en question les principes d'un modèle de développement fondé sur un système de production et d'échanges dépassé qui, non seulement s'avère aujourd'hui inadéquat aux exigences de la révolution technologique, mais s'est révélé au cours du XXe siècle tragiquement désastreux. Le capitalisme impérialiste est en effet aux sources non seulement de la pauvreté toujours plus extrême du Tiers-Monde, mais de la famine qui y sévit, comme il est la cause des deux guerres mondiales et celle, aussi sûre quoique moins immédiatement évidente, de presque toutes les guerres régionales. Sans compter qu'il est aussi responsable de l'endettement de toutes les économies nationales, des riches comme des pauvres, endettement impossible à surmonter et qui tient toutes les sociétés au bord du gouffre d'une troisième guerre mondiale, encore une fois seule porte de sortie de l'oligarchie qui commande le système et en profite.

Devant cet état de fait et à mesure que s'aggrave et s'amplifie la crise qui est l'aboutissement global (car affectant solidairement la totalité du globe) d'un processus ininterrompu de sur-exploitation des richesses humaines et naturelles dont le dernier avatar en liste est une pollution destructrice de notre environnement terrestre, processus encore, quoique dans une mesure toujours moindre, largement dominé par les États-Unis, ne devient-il pas absurde autant qu'inefficace de restreindre à ses seules conséquences économiques, la réflexion critique sur l'avenir de la société québécoise dans un cadre de libre-échange avec ce pays voisin?

Ne serait-il pas plus salutaire, particulièrement en ces jours d'hystérie financière où pouvoirs publics et médias tentent de nous faire vivre au rythme des accès de fièvre des cotes boursières, de nous interroger sur les moyens à prendre pour nous dépêtrer, plutôt que nous y enliser, de la déclinante organisation économico-politique américaine qui fonctionne sur l'exportation vers un marché mondial à la limite de la saturation et qui voudrait bien, par conséquent, envahir le nôtre sans aucune restriction, particulièrement avec ses biens culturels devenus son nouvel instrument de domination; qui fonctionne aussi, il importe de ne jamais le perdre de vue, sur la recherche militaire, sur la production et la vente d'armes de plus en plus coûteuses et meurtrières?

Ne serait-il pas plus fécond de profiter du débat suscité par la problématique du libre-échange, pour tenter

■■■■■■■■■■■■■■■■■■■■■■■■■■■■■■

d'élaborer dans toutes ses dimensions un projet de société qui nous libérerait de ce modèle de développement aussi néfaste que désuet?

Malheureusement, à prendre connaissance des nombreuses prises de position élaborées autant par les adversaires que par les partisans du projet d'accord, force est de constater que les deux camps produisent des analyses qui toutes également relèvent du même système de références. Pas plus les uns que les autres, en effet, ne remettent fondamentalement en question la pertinence, la validité et la légitimité de l'ordre établi, comme si tous également le considéraient de droit divin ou fondé en raison, alors qu'issu de la révolution industrielle, il n'est qu'historique et parfaitement arbitraire.

Avec le résultat que partisans et adversaires discourent comme s'ils n'avaient pas vraiment pris conscience des transformations majeures opérées dans nos sociétés capitalistes, comme s'ils ne voyaient pas qu'elles sont devenues des sociétés décisionnelles de moins en moins fondées sur la propriété privée des moyens de production, mais sur leur contrôle exercé conjointement par les gestionnaires de l'État, du marché et du savoir; comme s'ils n'avaient pas vraiment pris conscience que la révolution technologique, tout en ne faisant pas disparaître le capital et le travail comme forces productives importantes, les a toutefois remplacés par les sciences et les techniques comme moteur principal du développement économique, social et culturel des nations.

Nous pouvons ainsi voir notre récente fournée nationale d'industriels et de commerçants et leurs porte-parole: les Bourassa et les Parizeau (manifestement atteint du syndrôme de la tête à Papineau) s'imaginer que le libre-échange leur donne enfin la chance d'accomplir leur propre révolution bourgeoise, sans comprendre qu'elle est bel et bien révolue et qu'ils arrivent 150 ans trops tard pour en faire leur profit.

Ainsi en est-il des adversaires du libre-échange et particulièrement des chefs syndicaux. Ils proposent des stra-

■■■■■■■■■■■■■■■■■■■■■■■■■■■■■■■■

tégies de lutte qui ne tiennent généralement pas compte des modifications majeures opérées dans les rapports sociaux de force par les transformations du mode de production. Ils continuent à se battre comme s'ils avaient affaire aux propriétaires des moyens de production, sans voir que l'issue des luttes ne dépend plus d'un quelconque rapport réel des forces en présence, que les conflits, au contraire, trouvent de plus en plus rarement leurs solutions au terme d'affrontements ou de négociations entre les parties directement impliquées, mais qu'ils se règlent plutôt par concertation transversale entre les gestionnaires des diverses instances du pouvoir dont les solutions visent toujours à adapter le fonctionnement des entreprises aux besoins prioritaires de l'ordre économique mondial. C'est pourquoi il est vain pour les travailleurs de s'opposer au libre-échange en invoquant le spectre des pertes d'emplois, car, à l'intérieur du système actuel, accord ou non, ils disparaîtront. Il serait beaucoup plus efficace de contribuer à la prise de conscience de l'urgence de créer un nouveau modèle de développement.

D'où la nécessité absolue pour toutes les forces vives de la société québécoise, c'est-à-dire les forces qui ne visent pas uniquement le profit comme raison universelle de vivre, d'axer leur lutte contre le libre-échange sur la recherche de moyens propres à nous permettre de transformer en forces collectives favorables à notre épanouissement national et social, les multiples possibilités de développement humain que recèle la révolution technologique si nous nous organisons pour la maîtriser, plutôt que de nous laisser organiser par ceux qui la contrôlent déjà trop. Laissons nos capitalistes indigènes s'essouffler derrière leur rêve de révolution bourgeoise. Pour nous, tâchons de ne pas rater la révolution technologique, en l'enracinant dans notre langue et notre culture, dans nos aspirations vers une société équitable, pacifique et écologique.

■■■■■■■■■■■■■■■■■■■■■■■■■■■■■■■■

"The bully Canadians!"

Allan Fotheringham

---

*Allan Fotheringham, born in Hearn, Saskatchewan, is now
columnist for Southam News in Washington, D.C. One of
Canada's most brilliant pundits, he pontificates weekly in*
Maclean's *magazine.*

---

*Well, gee, I can't get a handle at all on this free trade
fuss.*

Do not agitate the inner recesses of your cranium. It
ain't going anywhere.

*But I thought this was to be the crowning achievement
of Mulroney's first term?*

He also thought he was safe as Houses with 211 seats,
but that hasn't done him much good.

But I thought each side had signed the deal?

Only the negotiators have signed anything. It still must
pass the House of Commons and Congress. It's called
democracy.

■■■■■■■■■■■■■■■■■■■■■■■■■■■■■■■■

Are you trying to tell me the Tories can't get it through the Commons with their huge majority?

You can't get anything through if public opinion turns against you. Canadian public opinion is now becoming very suspicious of the whole schmere.

Why is that?

Because the Tories tried to conduct the talks with the Americans in such secrecy that there arose the niggling feeling they were trying to hide something.

Were they?

Of course. We are only now learning some of the trade-offs the Tories were willing to make. It's why they've slipped to 23 per cent in the Gallup – a poll taken after they'd signed this supposedly historic pact.

Why are you so suspicious?

Born that way, luckily. Mother's fault. She taught me always to be wary about getting into bed with an elephant.

Don't you like Mr. Mulroney?

I'm a good friend, as a matter of fact. Especially when Mila is around. It's just that he suffers from one illusion.

What's that?

Mulroney was born and raised in Baie Comeau, Que., an artificial town built by the *Chicago Tribune* solely as a source of newsprint.

What's wrong with that?

Nothing. But Mr. Mulroney's father's job – and the baby's shoes – were as a result of American paternalism. He grew up thinking of Americans as providers.

Seems reasonable to me.

Shut up and listen. Later, Mulroney became president of Iron Ore Co. of Canada, a branch plant of Hanna Mining of Cleveland, which provided him with an executive jet and an apartment over Central Park in New York and lots of goodies.

Nothing wrong with that.

Nothing at all. But Mulroney has grown from a pup to a mature man with the belief – natural – that Americans are terribly nice people.

■■■■■■■■■■■■■■■■■■■■■■■■■■■■■■

Aren't they?

Of course they are, when taken individually. It's just that, in the mass, they control the world, and the elephant sometimes is rather clumsy in dealing with the mouse.

For example?

For example, the United States now controls 95 per cent of the film distribution in Canada, a near-monopoly that Culture Czar Flora MacDonald is now trying to dilute by nervously attempting to manoeuvre a bill past the business-minded neanderthals in the Tory cabinet. And Hollywood, catching the attention of its Hollywood president, is screaming discrimination. The bully Canadians!

You sound agitated.

No, just sad that a government with 208 seats can so misread the general feeling of Canadians.

How so?

Canadians were not told that their resources, especially water, were on the bargaining table. We were told that automobiles were not on the bargaining table. In fact, they were. We now know that Washington, at least until the final twenty-four hours, wanted a clause guaranteeing that Ottawa would pass the drug patent bill that would protect the U.S. multinationals. In other words, Washington would be telling Ottawa what laws to pass.

You're getting upset again.

Hardly. At any rate, all this could be avoided if Mulroney would phone me for advice.

45

"... what we have trundling into our community is a gimcrack Wooden Horse."

Graeme Gibson

Graeme Gibson is a Canadian novelist, his latest novel being Perpetual Motion. *As a long-time activist in cultural politics, he is one of the key figures in establishing better conditions for writers in Canada. Gibson is a founder of the Writers Union of Canada.*

The mind supplies the idea of a nation, but what gives that idea its sentimental force is a community of dreams. ANDRE MALRAUX

What "community of dreams" is evoked by the phrase "Canada is open for business"? Compare it, if you will, to "Canada *does* business." Obviously the latter statement is affirmative, that is to say, active; in contrast, our government's slogan reveals an alarming passivity.

One can't help feeling it is a passivity characteristic of branch-plant managers, or of those who have often failed

46

■■■■■■■■■■■■■■■■■■■■■■■■■■■■■■■

in their attempts to compete in the world. If they did not fear failure, surely they would not fear the need to diversify our trading base? If they do not fear diversification, why do they want to put all our eggs in the American basket?

Have they negotiated this deal out of that passivity?

In 1978 I was in Edinburgh when the people of Scotland narrowly rejected Devolution; that is, they refused the chance to establish a Scottish Assembly – one that would have had real but acceptably modest powers.

Opponents of Devolution, and there were many, stuffed glossy leaflets through my mailbox that said VOTE NO FOR SCOTLAND. As we know, the Scots eventually did that.

As a Canadian, who takes regional and provincial jurisdictions for granted, I was astonished and perplexed. How could the Scots, who after all still manage to consider themselves a nation, who frequently seem more confident about it than some Canadians are about this country, how and why did they let it happen?

This isn't the place to try to address what is a most complicated question, and I don't have clear answers, but several possibilities suggest themselves. To begin with, I believe that the intellectual and creative community failed to make clear what was at issue beneath the hectoring and political rhetoric. As a result the question was never properly debated.

More importantly, and at the heart of the matter, was a colonized people's conviction that they were incapable of resolving the problems of their community. It was easier to blame England for Scotland's woes, to blame Westminster, than to mobilize the faith and talent necessary to make Scotland work better. That is to say, if Scots had insisted on an Assembly, they would have had to accept responsibility for themselves and their country. In short, they were afraid. . . .

At least they were allowed to vote on the question!

My dismay at the prospect of our government's ''free trade'' deal has little to do with the debates over who is

■■■■■■■■■■■■■■■■■■■■■■■■■■■■■■■

right in the predictions about the number of jobs to be gained or lost. To begin with, like most Canadians, I don't believe the experts on either side know what they're talking about. How could they when, at this writing, few details have been hammered out and none has been revealed?

What really is this bit of bottom-land they're trying to sell, this bridge in Brooklyn, this pig in a poke? If you don't buy it you're a coward; if you even question the deal you're a fascist liar and troublemaker. I am one of those who suspects that what we have trundling into our community is a gimcrack Wooden Horse. . . . Inside it? Well now, yes, that's a good question. There are jobs inside: Jobs-Jobs-Jobs. No, you mustn't examine it too closely, not yet. We can't show it to you until its established in the city. But you can trust us. Haven't we promised you jobs before? So trust us, eh?

The fact is we aren't going to know what we're getting into or what's getting into us, and at what cost, until the deal is done.

Who in their right mind does business this way?

What we can say is that the current aggressive defence of "free trade" is overwhelmingly economic, as if money has taken priority over everything else. Apart from the lack of reference to the advantages of a benign climate, the argument suspiciously resembles those offered by Canadians after they have decided to live and work in the United States.

The relentless conviction of those who assert we must have free trade or die as a nation suggests a melancholy lack of faith in this country, and a woeful ignorance of what Canada, or any country, is.

That man who thinks only of harvests, has no memory.
What he has forgotten doesn't exist.
                         "Lady with Chains" by Roch Carrier

You seldom find this cultural and historical amnesia

■■■■■■■■■■■■■■■■■■■■■■■■■■■■■■■■

among, for example, artists and writers anymore; nor among athletes, research scientists, community activists, and all sorts of ordinary working men and women. Nor, by any means, do you find it throughout the business community.

In his wondrous book *Faces and Masks*, Eduardo Galleano quotes the nineteenth-century Cuban patriot Jose Marti – and since both revolutionary Cuba and the anti-Castro Cubans celebrate Marti we can record his remarks without fear of ideological *ad hominems*: "Whosoever says economic union, says political union. The people that buys gives the orders. The people that sells, serves. . . . The people that wants to die sells to one people alone, and the people that wants to save itself, sells to more than one. . . . The people that wants to be free distributes its business among equally strong peoples."

We live in a country that has stumbled and struggled, in fits and starts, toward various forms of collective decency. For many reasons, not all of our own making, we've managed to cultivate a "playing field" that recognizes, among other things (albeit imperfectly), that expenditures on social programs and equalization payments are preferable, for example, to expenditures on arms.

Is it therefore immodest or foolish to assert that if we actually are going to negotiate "a level playing field" with the Americans (where does one suppose the home advantage is going to lie?), that we insist our architects understand the kind of game we're trying to play up here?

■■■■■■■■■■■■■■■■■■■■■■■■■■■■■■

"Many of our children will grow up thinking that they are voting for a president. Maybe they really will."

Michele Landsberg

Michele Landsberg is a Toronto-born journalist and author. She has written the definitive Canadian guide to children's literature. A winner of two National Newspaper Awards, she currently writes a column from New York for The Globe and Mail.

Americans smile in polite mystification when I try to tell them why I'm against free trade. When I splutter about Canadian identity, even my most progressive friends wear a look of pitying attention: to them, as to Simon Reisman, mine is the sulky obduracy of a child who clings to a tattered security blanket. That scrap, their smiles say to me, makes me look defensive, pitiable. It's a feeble flag of vulnerability and weakness. Grow up! Play with the big boys!

Sometimes they almost convince me. Challenged to write "what I would tell my children about Canada," my first unbidden thought was of the streak of envious spite that many of us inherited from Britain and that was the dominant tone of the Canada of my youth. I grew up under the Canadian rubric of "None is too many," Canada's disgusting response to the pleas of Jews fleeing Nazis. "Too clever by half," Canadians would sneer about talkative, ambitious immigrants. We boast now about the distinctiveness of French Canada, but my high school history books taught me that "we English" won because the French were bumbling, treacherous, and corrupt.

Everything about the Canada of my childhood was prissy, ungenerous, xenophobic, pallid, and conformist.

What's to defend?

From my temporary vantage point in New York, the answer becomes clearer to me. We have a political culture to defend. From a weird blend of prairie populism, the British parliamentary system, and a deeply conservative legacy of values – duties and commitments, rather than free-booting individual rights – we somehow evolved into a country that leaves room for the democratic left.

When I try to explain the Canadian difference to my American friends, I find myself reciting the litany of the left. What irony: it's only here in New York that it strikes me how we have democratic socialists to thank for nearly everything that makes Canada distinctive – the CBC, the National Film Board, the farm marketing boards, unemployment insurance, paid maternity leave, and, above all, medicare. Successive Liberal and Conservative governments have sold us piecemeal down the river to foreign owners and masters. But thanks to that web of communication and collective responsibility, spun by the democratic left, most of us still feel like Canadians. We have a different view of the world; our news, films, songs, books, and radio programs – our whole tradition of non-commercial culture – keep it that way. Our children's musicians, authors, and television performers are a dazzling astonishment to Americans: they have no idea how we came up with such excellence. The answer is that public broadcasting formed our expectation of high

■■■■■■■■■■■■■■■■■■■■■■■■■■■■■■■

standards, immune to the consumer buck, in the entertainment we provide for our children. Is it embarrassing
that Canadian identity should somehow be linked to
gentle Mr. Dress-Up? True, nonetheless.

In mass-market America, there is no room for social
democracy and there never has been. Irresponsible and
macho in foreign policy as in Saturday morning cartoons,
Americans bow to the single imperative of the dollar.

Americans don't have a single left-wing member of
Congress. When a passion for social change wells up –
civil rights, the movement against the Vietnam War, the
popular sentiment for an Equal Rights Amendment – it
must storm Congress from the outside, and often with
futility. Our parliamentary tradition, in contrast, offers a
range of political choices that more accurately reflects
the electorate. Because there's a solid representation in
Parliament for dissenting views, we're not rocked and
battered between simplistic and irresponsible extremist
movements. Because we're "little guys" in population
and wealth, we have a modest and moderate stance
toward the rest of the world. We don't aim to bestride the
world like a Colossus. We conciliate. The world cher-
ishes us for that, and that, too, will be sucked up by the
American vortex when the border is ray-gunned into
oblivion.

The free trade advocates think that money is a separate
good that will flow across borders at no political or social
cost. They glibly promise, and as easily believe, that
culture will be "exempt." But we who are more deeply
committed to that culture are hypersensitive. We've already registered the ominous rumblings from American
publishing, movie, and periodical interests. We know
that along with their money will come the irresistible
demand for the dismantling of our "unfairly subsidized"
theatre, orchestras, public broadcasting, artists, Film
Board, and periodical and book publishing industries.
And once that stream of information and art has dried
up, our distinctive viewpoint will wither, too.

Years ago, when I criticized commercial daytime

television, dozens of Canadian children wrote to me indignantly to protest that *The Brady Bunch*, a saccharine sitcom, "teaches us how good American families should live." Children soaked in American commercial television do not know that they are Canadians. They are disinherited of our collectivist tradition. Some of them already think they are entitled to one phone call when arrested, that "zed" is pronounced "zee," that they have First Amendment rights, a sacred right to carry guns, and should hate Commies everywhere. Many of our children will grow up thinking that they are voting for a president. Maybe they really will.

As free trade, like a tide, washes away at our cultural foundations, our political structures will inevitably crumble. That's what's so hard to get across to people. "Identity" sounds thin-blooded and abstract, compared to the brassy gleam of promised jobs and quick loot. It's human nature to take what seems tangible: Esau, his mouth watering, lightly sold his birthright to Jacob in return for a steaming pot of lentils. Only later did he groan. Beans are only worth beans, but our birthright is our future as a people. Conservationists speak urgently about "species diversity" and "genetic extinction." Healthy diversity is the planet's bulwark. When our political structures have gone, what makes us different will be extinguished; Canadians will have become extinct. Our political culture, with its social democratic alternative, is what made me a Canadian, made me proud and glad to be one, and what we will surely tragically lose.

■■■■■■■■■■■■■■■■■■■■■■■■■

«. . . il faut qu'une cause soit bien mauvaise pour que ceux qui y croient la défendent par autant de mensonges».

Laurent Laplante

---

*Laurent Laplante est présentement commentateur pour
l'émmission* Ici Québec *de Radio Canada. Il a été rédacteur
de l'Action Catholique, éditorialiste au* Devoir, *directeur
de l'Office d'Information du Québec, et secretaire
de la Commission Royale d'Enquête sur la Justice.
Il demeure à Québec.*

L'argument le plus puissant qu'on puisse opposer au
libre-échange, c'est sans doute l'amas de mensonges dont
on s'est servi pour nous le vendre. En effet, à force de se
faire raconter des sornettes par des gens qui ne peuvent
manifestement pas croire ce qu'ils nous disent, on par-
vient à une certitude dont il n'est plus possible de se
dépouiller: *il faut que ce projet de libre-échange soit bien
nocif pour qu'on le propose en termes aussi mensongers*.

Car, depuis le début et sans discontinuer, la négociation
sur le libre-échange a baigné dans la tromperie. Jamais
le débat n'est vraiment devenu public et transparent.

■■■■■■■■■■■■■■■■■■■■■■■■■■■■■

Jamais on n'a su ce que les Américains demandaient, pas plus qu'on n'a su ce que notre gouvernement considérait comme vital ou inaliénable. Jamais les propos de M. Mulroney, de Ms. Carney, de M. Clark, de M. Reisman n'ont été convergents et donc crédibles. Jamais la substance des études entreprises pour le compte du gouvernement canadien n'a été étalée devant la Chambre des communes ou devant l'opinion publique. Jamais les rencontres entre M. Mulroney et les premiers ministres des provinces n'ont débouché sur un exposé clair ou sur des rapports d'étape intelligibles.

Certains considéront cette brume comme une simple «restriction mentale» qu'on peut et qu'on doit même pardonner en période de négociations. Peut-être, d'ailleurs, auront-ils en partie raison. Passons donc aux tromperies plus caractérisées, aux mensonges grossiers et totalement illégitimes. Pourquoi répéter que le pacte de l'auto n'est pas négociable et n'a pas été négocié quand on sait le contraire? Ce n'est pas pour tromper ou dérouter le négociateur adverse, puisque lui sait à quoi s'en tenir. Pourquoi affirmer péremptoirement que l'agriculture aussi est intouchable, quand l'inverse est vrai et quand le négociateur d'en face le sait mieux que le public canadien? Pourquoi, surtout, prétendre au son des trompettes qu'on a obtenu – contrairement à Israël – la création d'un véritable mécanisme neutre pour arbitrer les litiges canado-américains, alors qu'il n'en est rien?

Ce dernier élément mérite, tant il étonne et scandalise, qu'on insiste lourdement. À bien lire le projet de texte, on s'aperçoit, en effet, qu'*Ottawa et Washington n'ont pas convenu d'un arbitrage, mais d'un simple examen supplémentaire*. Rien de moins, mais surtout rien de plus. Si litige il y a, deux représentants de chacun des deux pays (plus une cinquième personne très probablement choisie *au hasard!*) vérifieront si la décision litigieuse a été prise en conformité avec les lois du pays où elle s'est élaborée. On vérifiera, par exemple, si les Américains se sont conformés aux lois *américaines* ont décrétant

■■■■■■■■■■■■■■■■■■■■■■■■■■■■■■■■

déloyale la commercialisation que font les Canadiens de leur bois de cèdre, de leur bois de construction ou de leur potasse. Si le verdict américain n'est pas *ultra vires* de la législation américaine, les Américains réagiront comme bon leur semblait et comme bon leur semble toujours. On peut parier sans risque que cette réaction américaine continuera à prendre la forme de droits compensatoires. Contrairement à ce que le public imagine lorsqu'on lui promet un véritable «mécanisme d'arbitrage» strictement personne ne pourra décréter que la législation américaine est protectionniste. Contrairement à ce qu'on nous répète à satiété, le protectionnisme américain pourra maintenir ses privilèges léonins pour peu que ses exigences se soient déployées conformément à la légalité américaine.

Répétons-le: il faut qu'une cause soit bien mauvaise pour que ceux qui y croient la défendent par autant de mensonges. Autant de tromperie conduit même à une conséquence regrettable: les adversaires du libre-échange ont devant eux tant de mauvaise foi qu'ils en viennent eux-mêmes à nier les éléments avantageux, pourtant réels et nombreux, d'une telle libéralisation des échanges. Ce qui achève de plonger l'opinion publique dans le désarroi.

Tout cela, remarquons-le, concerne le Canada entier. Le Québec, pour sa part, même réintégré dans la Confédération canadienne, peut-être même surtout à cause de cette réintégration, élabore présentement, face au libre-échange, sa méfiance propre, une méfiance décuplée.

En moins de cinq ans, le Québec a été tour à tour exclus de la confrérie canadienne, puis invité à y revenir. Comme les autres provinces canadiennes, il lui a fallu s'habituer à une vie politique nettement différente et où le pouvoir judiciaire, armé de la charte des droits, commence à ressembler au pouvoir judiciaire américain. Cet apprentissage, que toutes les provinces trouvent exigeant, fut d'autant plus exigeant pour le Québec que le Québec s'est trouvé soumis aux nouvelles règles sans en avoir jamais signé l'adoption. C'est une chose que de vivre selon une nouvelle constitution, c'en est une autre que

Laurent Laplante

■■■■■■■■■■■■■■■■■■■■■■■■■■■■■■■

d'obéir à une entente qu'on n'a pas entérinée. Cette «nuit des longs couteaux», le Québec ne sait pas encore, quoique puisse en dire Robert Bourassa, s'il l'a pardonnée ou s'il l'a inscrite dans un subconscient à base de «je me souviens».

Le projet du lac Meech, il est vrai, tente de convertir en mariage ce qui ressemblait, récemment encore, à un divorce. Les Québécois, dans l'ensemble, accueillent raisonnablement bien l'invitation à se joindre au groupe confédéral, mais ils notent quand même que le «party» a commencé bien avant leur venue et que leur arrivée ne déclenche pas partout des cris d'enthousiasme. Les Québécois remarquent aussi, avec passablement d'inconfort, que le projet du lac Meech a été tardivement et discrètement accepté au petit matin par onze hommes blêmes d'insomnie: piteuse démocratie, en effet, qui redoute à ce point le débat public. . . .

Dans ce contexte, Québec a toutes les raisons du monde de s'interroger sur la portée future d'un accord de libre-échange. L'incertitude, en effet, existe désormais à tous les niveaux, à tous les carrefours. Québec ne sait pas encore si l'accord du lac Meech sera ratifié. Québec ne sait pas quelle sera l'interprétation judiciaire d'un éventuel accord. Et Québec sait encore moins s'il peut compter sur le pouvoir central du Canada pour faire valoir la «spécificité québécoise» face au rouleau-compresseur américain.

Québec, *mutatis mutandis*, peut-il croire, par exemple, qu'Ottawa va tenir tête aux *majors* américains et les obliger au respect des francophones? Québec n'a-t-il pas raison de redouter qu'on le *donne* pour obtenir autre chose des Américains? Comment, en effet, espérer qu'Ottawa exigera des Américains le respect de la spécifité québécoise quand il ne l'a encore respectée lui-même ni dans la formation des équipes olympiques, ni dans le transport public, ni dans les services de la GRC, ni dans le recrutement et le fonctionnement de la fonction publique . . .?

Québec n'a pas encore la preuve qu'Ottawa l'a déjà

■■■■■■■■■■■■■■■■■■■■■■■■■■■

donné, mais il a eu cent fois la preuve que les négociateurs fédéraux, à l'intérieur comme à l'extérieur du pays, le considéraient comme menu fretin. D'où une vaste méfiance attisée par la soudaineté des multiples virages récemment effectués en pleine noirceur.

■■■■■■■■■■■■■■■■■■■■■■■■■■■■■■
"Business goals are one thing.

The future of Canada

is quite another."

Frank Stronach

Frank Stronach is chairman of the board and chief executive officer of Magna International Inc. in Markham, Ontario. Magna designs, develops, and manufactures automotive components and systems. Magna employs over 10,000 people and had consolidated sales in 1986 in excess of one billion dollars.

As a corporate officer, I should begin by noting that this proposed free trade agreement could be advantageous to Magna. But as a private citizen concerned with achieving a fairer and more productive society, I have some concerns with this agreement. Business goals are one thing. The future of Canada is quite another.

This deal may be quite beneficial to business – especially to multinational corporations. Economies of scale benefit the owners of business. But greater returns to business might not necessarily be in the best interests of the country. Money has no heart, no soul, no conscience,

■■■■■■■■■■■■■■■■■■■■■■■■■■■■■■

and it knows no boundaries. Business is driven by short-term gains. As a country, though, we must look down the road at the long-term effect. Trading should be encouraged but it must relate to jobs. To do this effectively we require a national industrial strategy.

Many multinational corporate leaders in Canada might like to see an end to trade restrictions. It makes the job easier for them. In the case of Magna, it certainly would make my job easier. But we must ask, ''Who speaks for Canada?'' Foreign-based multinationals? I do not think so.

The political, social, and economic fabrics of our country – of any country – are closely interwoven. The political and economic fabrics determine and shape the social fabric. As a result, this free trade agreement could ultimately affect the society and culture of Canada. If our economy becomes too closely integrated with the American economy, our culture and our society will likewise become more identified with American culture and society. That is not necessarily bad. However, we as a country might want to do things differently. Therefore, any agreement to improve trade must not preclude us from having the ability to make those unique economic decisions we consider imperative to determining our national future. Only then can we hope to achieve a fairer and more productive society.

■■■■■■■■■■■■■■■■■■■■■■■■■■■■
"Global economics is driving
us into this crazy situation."

David Takayoshi Suzuki

---

*David Suzuki is one of Canada's most widely known
geneticists and broadcasters. For more than ten years his* The
Nature of Things *on* CBC *television has helped make
Canadians more aware of the role of science in our lives.*

Polls indicate that Canadians value wilderness and a clean
environment and they are willing to pay for it through
increased taxes. Yet many of those same people maintain that we must do everything we can to stimulate
steady growth in the economy, consumer goods, and
income. Upon reflection, it is clear these are not mutually
sustainable goals. For it is industrial growth and development that are the very *cause* of environmental degra-
dation and wilderness loss.

Nothing illustrates better our failure to grapple with our
contradictory beliefs than the current debate over free
trade with the United States. Supporters and opponents

■■■■■■■■■■■■■■■■■■■■■■■■■■■■■■■■

of free trade alike begin their arguments from the *same assumption* – the absolute necessity of steady economic growth. The disagreement is merely over *how*. Yet by failing to question the underlying assumptions, we assure that regardless of what we do, two of the planet's most pressing problems – environmental pollution and the decrease in biological diversity through species extinction – will continue unabated.

Perhaps the most pernicious notion we live with today is the sanctity of economic growth. We measure "progress" by the increase in income, trade, and goods. Steady economic growth from year to year is a pattern called "exponential growth" and every politician, business person, and economist assume its necessity. Not only is it an impossible goal, it is leading us to global disaster.

Suppose we plot the per capita consumption of air, water, land and resources, production of pollution, habitat destruction, and species extinction. Over the entire course of human history, the curves are virtually flat for 99 per cent of that time. Equilibrium, stasis, and balance with the rest of nature have been the normal human condition. Only in recent centuries have the curves begun to climb visibly upward; in this century, they all become nearly vertical as they leap off the top of the page.

Pro-free-traders speak about the devastating consequences for Canada if a deal with the U.S. is not achieved. We just have to have the markets, it is argued, to sustain growth in our economy or we stagnate. But suppose all the rest of the world disappeared today, leaving only Canada. Would we be plunged into a famine? Of course not, for we are one of the few breadbaskets left in the world. Would we freeze in the cold? Not when we are so rich in petroleum and hydro power. Would we be forced to live in tents and caves when we have such vast forests for lumber? The fact is, we are a country that is the envy of most people on this planet when it comes to resources. Yet somehow, we are now told, we are a nation about to "go under" without the opportunities of an American market.

Global economics is driving us into this crazy situation. It rests on a completely human-created notion of *value* based on money. The idea is so artificial that people can actually become wealthy merely by manipulating numbers in a stock exchange while contributing *absolutely nothing* to the world in the process. Third World countries destroy agriculture, forests, and marine resources vital to their own survival for quick cash returns from coffee, hardwood lumber, cheap beef, and anchovies. The global marketplace generates a terrible dependence that further impoverishes the already destitute and leads rich countries like Canada to sell off energy and forests that should be retained for future generations – all for the immediate benefits of dollars.

■■■■■■■■■■■■■■■■■■■■■■■■■■■■■■■

"Canadians believe that we are responsible for one another, that life is survival for all, not just for the fittest."

Bob White

Bob White is president of the Canadian Auto Workers Union and Canada's most celebrated and controversial labour leader. He came to Canada from Ireland in 1949 and lives in Toronto.

We have built a country vastly different from the U.S. because generations of Canadians have had a vision of a caring, decent, and fair-minded society.

Canadians have a medical system that guarantees everyone good health care, not just those who can afford it. We have social programs that address the needs of the elderly, the needy, the homeless, and the sick. Canadians believe that we are responsible for one another, that life is survival for all, not just for the fittest.

We have a flourishing multicultural environment. Our cities are safe. Our citizens live in security.

Free trade threatens these achievements because it

■■■■■■■■■■■■■■■■■■■■■■■■■■■■■■■■

means eventually accepting the social standards of a country that:

- has not yet introduced universal medicare and whose social programs generally rank last among industrialized countries;
- has the lowest proportion of unionized workers in the industrialized West;
- has the weakest limits on what corporations can and cannot do in the public interest.

It's no accident that the Business Council on National Issues is in the forefront regarding the free trade deal. A cabal of 150 companies, many U.S.-owned, with assets of $725 billion, the Council has never shied away from protecting the interests of the multinationals.

The truth is that moving Canada toward U.S. standards is exactly what the major business groups have been seeking for years. Free trade will do it for them by putting pressure on Canadian jobs. With jobs threatened, the pressure to roll back or limit our social programs will be intensified in the name of "competitiveness."

Any attempt to build a better society by improving social programs – developing adequate childcare; extending medicare; improving pensions and unemployment insurance; tax reform; equal pay for work of equal value – will be attacked as undermining our competitiveness. In essence there will be a ceiling on what we can achieve. That ceiling will be what exists in the United States.

Free trade will also limit our ability to create a made-in-Canada, made-for-Canadians economy because free trade is not just about the actual agreement but about its consequences as well. Most of the tariffs between our two countries are already low or about to be lowered by international agreement. Consequently, the free trade issue is really about so-called "non-tariff barriers," which include just about anything that interferes with the market. As a result, our economic policies could be affected.

Such policies as encouraging more Canadian processing of resources, assuring Canadian content, or using

■■■■■■■■■■■■■■■■■■■■■■■■■■■■■■■■

regional grants to develop new industries will be contrary to "free" trade because their purpose is to intervene in the market. We would therefore find ourselves in a double bind: any policies that successfully brought jobs to Canada would be attacked by U.S. business as unfair competition, as a violation of free trade. And any attempts to make progress in Canada on social programs would be attacked by Canadian business as making us uncompetitive.

It's important to remember that we have managed to survive as a unique culture in spite of our closeness to the U.S. giant. But much of our uniqueness depends on our social programs and other forms of government intervention that create a more compassionate, caring society than the highly individualistic credo of the U.S. allows. Free trade poses a severe if not devastating threat to this generous tradition, a tradition generations of Canadians have willingly paid the price for. And it will mean the loss of an important source of our unique identity in North America.

Prime Minister Mulroney is prepared to give all that up for the sake of a very weak agreement that does not even satisfy his original requirements for a "good" deal. Mulroney said going into the free trade talks that, at minimum, he was seeking guarantees from the U.S. that Canadian products would have unlimited access to the U.S. and that the U.S. would agree to not impose retaliatory tariffs on our goods. He also wanted a binding mechanism to settle disputes.

He lost on all counts. Access to the U.S. market is not guaranteed. Countervailing tariffs, such as those recently imposed on potash and softwood lumber, are not prohibited. And as for the disputes settlement mechanism, Canada can only appeal after an objectionable U.S. tariff has been imposed; and the U.S. has only to prove that it did not violate its own trade laws.

But to get this very, very shaky deal, Mulroney had to surrender much of Canada's sovereignty. We have lost

■■■■■■■■■■■■■■■■■■■■■■■■■■■■■■■

the right to control our energy supply. We have lost the right to design cultural policies without reference to the U.S. We have lost the right to control foreign investment. We have lost the ability to design national economic strategies. We have restricted our ability to formulate independent trade policies with other countries. We have lost the right to determine an independent auto strategy. These areas of decision-making are essential to even the most minimal definition of sovereignty.

Whatever concessions the Americans may have yielded in these areas are meaningless. The Americans simply don't have to worry about Canadian domination of their culture, economy, or resource sector. Furthermore, the tariffs the U.S. lowered were lower than Canada's anyway. It's small wonder that Ronald Reagan has hailed this deal as a new economic constitution for North America parallelling the Constitution of the U.S. founding fathers.

In the face of the most serious political question to come along in our country for decades, the ruling Conservative Party is resorting to name-calling as a central defence of the free trade agreement. Most of us are familiar with the outbursts of Canada's chief negotiator, Simon Reisman. But the Prime Minister, too, as well as cabinet ministers and spokespersons from the business lobby are calling free trade opponents ''cowards'' who have ''no confidence'' in Canada's ability to compete under free trade.

The truth is that free trade opponents are not opposed because we do not have enough confidence in Canada, but because we have so much. If free to pursue our own Canadian way, we can continue to build a healthy, decent, caring society despite our closeness to the U.S. – as we have for generations.

What We Know■■■■■■■■■■■■■■■■■

October 3, 19 87

PAY TO THE
ORDER OF   The United States of America $

_____ DOLLARS
                                    100

THE BANK OF CANADA
234 WELLINGTON ST.
OTTAWA, ONT. K1A 0G9

Brian Mulroney

KRIEGER©1987
THE PROVINCE

■■■■■■■■■■■■■■■■■■■■■■■■■■■■■■■■■

". . . the creation of 350,000 new jobs can be said to be based on highly speculative . . . assumptions . . ."

Peter Bakvis

Peter Bakvis is an economist at the Montreal-based Confédération des syndicats nationaux. *He is a representative to the International Labour Organization of the United Nations.*

While most Canadians would no doubt agree that the question of the impact on jobs should be a primary determinant as to whether or not Canada enter into a free trade agreement, there appears to be no automatic consensus on this question among economic specialists, even among those working on a government level.

Most of the sectoral studies carried out by the industry and commerce departments of the federal, Ontario, and Quebec governments or by the former Department of Regional Industrial Expansion arrived at quite negative conclusions as to the impact of free trade on jobs. The Quebec government study, for example, concluded that among Quebec's manufacturing industries, the free trade "losers" employ eight times as many workers as do the "winners."

A completely different appreciation of the impact of free trade on jobs is given by the general economic projections carried out by the Economic Council of Canada (ECC). Prime Minister Mulroney and other free trade proponents regularly cite the ECC's latest projections, released in August, which claim that free trade between Canada and the United States will create from 189,000 to 350,000 new jobs from now till 1995.

The apparent discrepancy between these studies can be largely explained by the assumptions on which they are based. The former sectoral studies try to isolate the effect of free trade on specific industries by assuming no significant changes in general economic conditions. The ECC's econometric study tries to measure the general impact of free trade on the Canadian economy, but in order to do so it makes some fairly audacious assumptions about changes in the economy and about what free trade will entail.

Given the wide extent to which the ECC study is referred to in support of the October 3 free trade agreement, it would seem worthwhile to compare the Council's assumptions with what is actually included in the free trade accord. There are in fact major differences between the two, something that free trade supporters either seem not to be aware of or choose to ignore.

One of the major assumptions on which the ECC projections are based is that services be completely *excluded* from a free trade accord. In fact, the October 3 agreement includes a provision on the principles to be applied in a sector-by-sector liberalization in services, with detailed arrangements to be included in the final text and aimed at covering architecture, tourism, telecommunications, computer services, and, possibly, transportation. The October 3 agreement also includes liberalization of financial services.

■■■■■■■■■■■■■■■■■■■■■■■■■■■■■■■■■■■■■■

The exclusion of services, which the ECC justifies by evoking measurement difficulties, is no minor detail. In its conclusions as to net job creation, fully 83 to 90 per cent of the jobs it forecasts would be created in services, the very sector the ECC assumes to be excluded from free trade.

The ECC's job-creation predictions may well have been very different and even negative if services were included. No less an authority than the pro-free trade Macdonald Commission concluded in 1985: "Overall it is likely that the United States has more to gain from the reciprocal reduction of barriers to trade in services than has Canada."

The ECC further makes the completely unrealistic assumption that under free trade all U.S. countervailing tariffs will disappear while Canadian subsidy programs, which are at the source of many U.S. countervails, remain untouched. The October 3 accord in fact explicitly stipulates that all existing U.S. countervails remain in place (as well as the special Canadian export tax on sawed lumber) and that U.S. trade laws that could give rise to new countervails on Canadian goods also remain in place.

While the accord does establish a working group that is supposed to propose a substitute regime to replace U.S. and Canadian trade laws by the mid-1990s, it could hardly be expected that such a new regime would leave Canada's subsidy programs entirely intact.

The ECC econometric model furthermore excludes by assumption all adjustment costs as well as the possibility that under free trade some U.S.-based corporations may decide to close their Canadian branch plants. But the most important premise, which is crucial to the scenario of 350,000 new jobs, is the arbitrary assumption that manufacturing productivity will increase by 6.1 per cent because of free trade and that 100 per cent of the productivity gain will be passed on to consumers in lower prices. Not only that, but the ECC also assumes that the elimination of tariffs on imports will also be entirely passed on to consumers.

Based on this highly optimistic scenario, the ECC calculates that over an eight-year period prices would fall (by 5.7 per cent) somewhat more than wages (which fall by 2.7 per cent). This additional 3 per cent purchasing power in the economy, plugged into the government's input-output model, translates into the 350,000 additional jobs.

One has only to change slightly the ECC model's basic assumptions to throw these projections completely askew. If, for example, one assumes that productivity growth due to free trade were only two-thirds of what the ECC arbitrarily assumes, and that prices were adjusted downward by only two-thirds of the increase in productivity and the elimination of tariffs, free trade would have virtually no effect on economic growth and jobs.

Despite these very major drawbacks, it would be unfair to dismiss the ECC's discussion paper on free trade as nothing more than some crudely disguised wishful thinking. The study does include detailed estimations of the value of tariff and some non-tariff barriers on manufacturing, barriers that will disappear with free trade. Its findings about Canadian manufacturing should be a rude awakening for many free trade advocates who imagined that free trade would lead to a huge increase of Canadian manufacturing exports to the U.S. The ECC clearly establishes that average Canadian trade barriers, notably tariffs, are higher than American barriers, with the result that their elimination will cause imports to rise more than exports, worsening Canada's current account balance.

It is unfortunate that what may have been a useful contribution of the ECC to the free trade debate has been completely overridden by the government's insistence on forcing the Council to make a comprehensive pronouncement on free trade's favourable impact on jobs. This

■ ■

pronouncement proclaiming the creation of 350,000 new jobs can be said to be based on highly speculative and, in some cases, completely incorrect assumptions as to how the Canadian economy works and as to what the free trade agreement includes.

"The history of free trade negotiations with the United States suggests that Canada's assets are too often given short shrift . . ."

Peter Baskerville

Peter Baskerville is a history professor at the University of Victoria in B.C. and a leading authority on public policy. He is the author of The Bank of Upper Canada.

Current affairs are not always what they seem. Sometimes only the publication of private diaries, the unearthing of confidential correspondence, or the release of restricted government documents gives electors real insight into the affairs of state. Certainly the history of Canadian-American relations, and especially Canadian-American trade relations, testifies to the reality of hidden agendas, mixed motives, and complex interrelations. A brief review of aspects of that history provides a perspective for evaluating current Canadian-American issues.

Canada's "birth" in 1867 is a case in point. It is often suggested that fear of American aggression spurred John

■■■■■■■■■■■■■■■■■■■■■■■■■■■■■■■■

A. Macdonald and other Canadian Fathers of Confederation to bury political hatchets and unite against a common threat. Orators such as Thomas D'Arcy McGee
warned Canadians that the acquisition of Canada was
"the first ambition of the American Confederacy."
McGee's warnings seemed confirmed by the actions of a
rag-tag group of Irish nationalists living in the United
States called Fenians, who believed that Britain could be
harmed by attacking her colonies. For a while the Canadian press and Canada's politicians seemed to see Fenians
behind every bush. Yet the reality was much more pro-
saic. And Macdonald knew it. A secret agent reported to
Macdonald at length concerning the division, poor leadership, and lack of organization that characterized the
Fenian "menace." In the end, as Macdonald well antic-
ipated, few battles occurred. But local hysteria was grist
for Macdonald's mill. Pro-confederationists used these
imagined threats to put down opposition. Defence, they
claimed, demanded British North American unity. To
oppose such unity was to be pro-American and anti-Brit-
ish. The War of 1812, when York (present-day Toronto)
had been twice sacked by the Americans, and the border
raids following the internal rebellions of 1837-38 were
still alive in many British North American memories and
provided the historical context for such rhetoric.

As early as 1867, then, Canada's politicians created
American images to suit their own purposes. Examples
of similar manipulation can be found in tracing Canadian
westward expansion following 1867 and, indeed, in the
building of that alleged engine of unity, the Canadian
Pacific Railway. Canada's politicians have been quick to
exploit the American presence to achieve their own
political/national ends. Relations of this sort, however,
did not require American signatures. How has Canada
fared when seated opposite the United States at bargaining tables on which trade and economic issues are prom-
inently placed?

In 1854 Upper and Lower Canada, as Ontario and

Quebec were then known, entered into a free trade or reciprocity agreement with the United States. What is interesting about this agreement is the refusal of Canadian negotiators to commit themselves to free trade in manufactured items. Agricultural and forest products appeared on the reciprocity lists; finished products did not. During the life of this treaty the importation of American manufactured goods declined, while trade in natural products increased. In 1858, when the Canadas instituted a tariff with high rates against the importation of manufactured goods, Americans cried that the treaty's spirit had been violated. The Canadians, in order to protect home industry from foreign competition and to raise needed revenue, held firm. For their part, American politicians pressured by similar indigenous industrial groups increased their tariffs and, when the Reciprocity Treaty came up for renewal in 1866, offered Canada free trade in unfinished millstones, grindstones, gypsum, firewood, and rags! The Canadians had the sense to decline. The treaty ended and for the rest of the nineteenth century high tariffs dominated Canadian/American commercial relations, just as they did relations between most other industrialized nations at that time.

In opting for high tariffs, Canada had little choice. Several times in the late nineteenth century the United States refused to consider Canadian reciprocity overtures. Americans were content with the status quo. Aggressive American manufacturers could and did hop across the tariff wall and set up branch plants in Canada. Consumers and industrialists in the United States tapped sufficient local American natural resources – wood, mineral, and agricultural products – to satisfy their immediate needs. Canada, on the other hand, somewhat naively welcomed all American branch plants with great glee. Other industrializing countries, such as Sweden, erected high tariffs and in strategic economic sectors also barred foreign competition. Canada's policy-makers lacked the notion of special sectors, and as a result American-owned

■■■■■■■■■■■■■■■■■■■■■■■■■■■■■■■■

industry quickly dominated central, high-growth, and technologically sophisticated manufacturing areas.

By 1906, American policy-makers came to the conclusion that such domination was insufficient. The reasons for change were clearly enunciated in a series of confidential high-level policy papers circulated within the upper echelons of the American government. This policy shift set the foundations for twentieth-century economic and commercial relations with Canada. It is, therefore, worth examining. American policy-makers believed that natural resources were becoming increasingly scarce and expensive in the United States at the very time when the manufacturing sectors had begun to produce more goods than locals could consume. Increased exports provided one solution to industrial over-expansion. But, the policy-makers warned, competition was fierce in world markets and would become even greater. Cheap inputs of raw material were therefore required to keep manufacturing and labour costs low enough to compete effectively in the world markets. In other words, Canada could supply rough lumber, iron ore, wheat, and other primary products and thereby aid the United States in its aim of dominating world trade. Given the extent of American control of Canada's industry, such an agreement would, as President William Howard Taft confided to former President Theodore Roosevelt in 1911, "make Canada only an adjunct of the United States." By separating Canada from British economic interests it would also weaken England, one of America's prime competitors in the area of world trade. The proposed agreement, Taft believed, truly represented "a parting of the ways."

Taft's enthusiasm for such a trade agreement rode roughshod over a proper sense of diplomatic circumspection and he voiced such sentiments publicly as well as privately. Not surprisingly, opponents of reciprocity in Canada took such quotes and effectively hammered the pro-reciprocity Wilfrid Laurier-led Liberal government. Intense fears of American domination – in this case not

■■■■■■■■■■■■■■■■■■■■■■■■■■■■■■■■■

at all paranoic – rose to the fore and reciprocity died a quick death.

American policy initiatives lived on, to resurface during the Depression of the 1930s. The negotiation of the path-breaking Canadian-American reciprocity agreement in 1935 was a truly incredible process that sheds light not just on the continuity of American policy but also on the duplicitous nature of some Canadian politicians concerning the American relationship. R.B. Bennett, Canada's Conservative Prime Minister, had tried to "blast" his way into world markets via a policy of retaliatory tariffs in the early 1930s. This initiative had failed and by 1935 Bennett was deep in negotiations with Americans over a free trade agreement. American negotiators operated from the premise, as one highly placed official wrote, that "there is still time, while [the] Canadian economy is in a formative stage, to stifle the emphasis away from highly competitive production to complementary production." [If we succeed in this it will] "have the long-range effect of bringing Canada not only within our economic but our political orbit."

Bennett bargained hard. He was reluctant to grant any concessions without receiving something meaningful in exchange. Partly for this reason, negotiations dragged on and Canadian voters booted Bennett out of office before the consummation of an agreement. The real reason for prolonging the negotiations, however, lay elsewhere. William Lyon Mackenzie King, leader of the opposition Liberal Party, secretly insinuated himself into the bargaining process. He confided to influential American government advisers that they could expect a better deal from him if they would only wait until his party defeated Bennett in the forthcoming election. At the same time, he suggested that the Americans could "hook" Bennett to favour free trade by continuing to negotiate with him. One American adviser believed that "the hooking" had worked wonderfully. Bennett had firmly, clearly, and

■■■■■■■■■■■■■■■■■■■■■■■■■■■■■■■

publicly committed himself to free trade. He could hardly oppose it following his defeat.

With King as Prime Minister negotiations went swiftly and smoothly. One American negotiator confided to President Franklin D. Roosevelt, ''the new set-up . . . is vastly more favourable to the United States than the one which was being considered with Mr. Bennett.'' After the signing, a U.S. State Department official characterized the results as ''staggering . . . so favourable to us that . . . it will be recognized generally as a great economic and political asset.'' Fêted and petted by American politicians and by the American President, King luxuriated in having, in his words, opted for the ''American road.'' What is problematic is less his choice of direction and more the means he employed to achieve it. Realistically, Canada by the late 1930s had little option but to cultivate American trade. Bennett realized this, but he tempered that realization with the belief that he led an autonomous country with strong assets that could be effectively employed in any commercial negotiations. In 1935, King, in his lust for the limelight and political power, overlooked all of that. He manipulated the American relationship to suit his own personal and party ends. Canada suffered from this failure in leadership.

King eventually may have come to a similar conclusion, at least subconsciously. During World War II, pressure for further continental integration was intense and, given war conditions, difficult to resist. As early as 1942 King began to realize the dangers associated with such integration. The Alaska Highway, he confided, ''was less intended for protection against the Japanese than as one of the fingers of the hand which America is placing more or less over the whole of the Western hemisphere.'' By 1948 King had decided that a further liberalization of trade would not be appropriate: it would assist the Americans in their desire to control ''all of North America.''

King was correct. The American ambassador urged that a further trade agreement be quickly effected as it

■■■■■■■■■■■■■■■■■■■■■■■■■■■■■■■■

would channel "the expansion of the Dominion's economy along lines complementary to that of the U.S."
America's assistant secretary of state for economic affairs
concurred. Such an agreement would facilitate "the most
efficient utilization of the resources of the North American continent and knitting the two countries together –
an objective of U.S. foreign policy since the founding of
the republic." Resources were the key. Even more than
before the war, Americans believed they were resource
poor and that their future in world trade depended on
replenishing the resource pot. Canada had the iron, cop-
per, tungsten, uranium, oil, and nickel that the United
States required. And, at least some American officials
believed that such resources were virtually theirs for the
asking.

The origins of America's post-World War II economic
policy vis-à-vis Canada extend back at least to 1906 and
are clearly revealed in 1935 and during World War II.
The ongoing attempts to implement these goals in the
decades following 1950 have had a major impact on
Canada's ability to act as an autonomous nation. The history of free trade negotiations with the United States suggests that Canada's assets are too often given short shrift
by Canadian politicians desirous of harnessing (albeit
fleetingly) the American eagle.

Kissin' Cousins

■■■■■■■■■■■■■■■■■■■■■■■■■■■■

"... 'job dislocations' ...

means ... that you or your

neighbour is about to become

unemployed."

Shirley Carr

Shirley Carr was the first woman to be elected leader of the Canadian Labour Congress. As president of the CLC, she is a member of the governing body of the International Labour Organization of the United Nations. She lives in Ottawa.

When Brian Mulroney talks about his free trade scheme with the United States, he sounds a bit like a undertaker. He speaks in mush words and euphemisms. When undertakers talk about somebody resting in the parlour they really mean somebody is dead. When Brian Mulroney talks about free trade he talks about "job dislocations" and what he really means is that you or your neighbour is about to become unemployed. What he is talking about is burying jobs and embalming dreams.

The time has come for the government to stop using the mush words and start being truthful in what it is say-

■■■■■■■■■■■■■■■■■■■■■■■■■■■■■■■

ing to Canadians. After all, we are talking about your livelihood and our children's livelihood.

Free trade is one of the most important challenges facing Canadians today. It not only threatens to gut our sovereignty like a salmon in a fish house, but it is primed to take the paycheque away from hundreds of thousands of Canadian workers. At the Canadian Labour Congress the Mulroney trade deal is looked on as nothing less than a corporate blueprint to plunder a nation's treasure house and snatch away the soul of its people.

Despite the government's best attempts to shy away from the truth and the real meaning of its trade plans with the Americans, there have been enough leaked government documents to know that this government has acted in bad faith. The government's own studies have shown that up to 800,000 Canadians face – to use the government's mush words – "job dislocation" if the trade deal goes through. That's 800,000 too many of our friends and neighbours on the bread lines.

Take a look at our textile industry. In the non-union southern U.S. there are single plants that produce enough towels in a week to do our country for an entire year. Given that kind of output, does Brian Mulroney really think the small Canadian mill town has a chance? And what about the workers in those towns? Our border towns could become ghost towns.

The future that Brian Mulroney and his Conservatives seem ready to carve out for Canada seems a far cry from the political war chant of "jobs, jobs, jobs" that he shouted across the land in the 1984 election campaign. Given the number of U.S. branch plants that have flourished under previous Canadian governments and the Tories' penchant for allowing an "anything-goes" investment policy from the United States, it seems a safe bet that with free trade there would be an exodus of industry from Canada.

The Economic Council of Canada predicted that as many as 350,000 new jobs would be created by free

■■■■■■■■■■■■■■■■■■■■■■■■■■■■■■■■■

trade. Unfortunately, these jobs – if they ever surface at all – seem to be primarily in the retail selling sector, in what Tory forecasters seem to think will be consumer buying frenzy to purchase cheaper U.S. goods.

The government seems ready to create minimum-wage jobs while intentionally forgetting the standard of living we now enjoy, which was created by higher-paying industrial manufacturing, service, transportation, and research jobs. Many of these would be gone with the Mulroney-Reagan trade deal. As for the minimum wage itself, don't look for it to stay at its present level. You can be sure the U.S. trade negotiators want it dropped to their level. The new buzzwords among Tory front and backbenchers are "efficiency" and "competitiveness." Translated into workplace jargon, this means "you are getting paid too much for what you do" – according to the corporate blueprint.

In the trade union movement we know that the economy is made up of people, and we want the government to wake up and realize that they are not just juggling statistics but people's lives. There are still people in this country who believe there is more to Canada than a corporate office tower.

The Tory government has brought in the concept of a so-called level playing field. To us, this level playing field is a dark design, and while it may be central to those who plot a free trade deal we are convinced that this idea will do Canada irreparable harm. Things are not level on both sides of the border. They are not equal. They never have been and we don't want them to be.

We fought for medicare and want to keep it. Even though it can be improved, we think our unemployment insurance plan is far superior to what the Americans offer their workers and we want to keep it. The trade union movement is not about to stand idly by while a government tries to dilute economic and social and political policies to the same watery consistency of the United States.

Before they were elected, Tories sang a different song

■■■■■■■■■■■■■■■■■■■■■■■■■■■■■■■

about free trade – and maybe that's why some Canadians believed them and voted for them. It wasn't that long ago that front-bench Tory David Crombie had a different view of free trade than he does today: "It's silly," he said. "Canada must improve relations with the United States, of course. But our national destiny is to become a global leader, not America's weak sister."

Michael Wilson whistled a far different tune before he became Finance Minister: "Bilateral free trade with the United States is simplistic and naive." Joe Clark even talked about great job losses due to free trade back in 1983.

And Brian Mulroney, before he met Ronald Reagan, claimed to be vehemently opposed to free trade. It was 1983 when he uttered these words – although it seems light years away now: "This country could not survive with a policy of unfettered free trade. This is a separate country. We'd be swamped. All that would happen with that kind of concept would be the boys cranking up their plants in bad times and shutting their entire branch plants in Canada. It's bad enough as it is."

But we say Canada has a choice. The labour movement believes that Canada does not have to be locked to the American economy and have the key thrown away. We know Canada is a trading nation and we have faith that we can tap into markets all around the world and not just south of the border. We have long been a proponent of free trade through multilateral negotiations. We believe we should redouble our efforts to increase exports to Europe, the Third World, and Pacific Rim. We also know it may not be easy to break into these markets, but then Canada didn't get where it is in the world today by taking the easy route.

Our future and our livelihood are at stake in the next little while. Our children deserve more of a shot at the future than a minimum-wage job at McDonald's – and maybe an American minimum wage at that.

"... our social and economic programs are in greater danger than ever before."

Marjorie Cohen

Marjorie Cohen is an economist who teaches at the Ontario Institute for Studies in Education. She has recently written a book on Free Trade and the Future of Women's Work. *Cohen is an activist in the Coalition Against Free Trade.*

The spectre of U.S. protectionism has haunted the Mulroney government. In the panic leading up to the free trade agreement, Canada's demands became minimal. The issue of a "binding disputes settlement mechanism" consumed discussion and appears to have become Canada's only real demand. We were told that if Canada could get this one feature our country could be rescued from U.S. protectionism. We would achieve what no other nation on earth had managed to get – exemption from the mighty power of U.S. trade legislation.

"Binding" was the operative word. Prime Minister Mulroney knew he had to come through on this or his

■■■■■■■■■■■■■■■■■■■■■■■■■■■■■■■■■

credibility would be shattered. And bound we are. We are bound to apply *American* law whenever U.S. firms want to challenge the way we do things in Canada. There has been no change in the rules.

If a U.S. firm feels its Canadian competitor is selling too cheaply or is able to sell at a lower cost because of some government program, it can sue before the U.S. International Trade Commission, as it has always been able to, on grounds of unfair trade practices. Then the new wrinkle. If the U.S. decision goes against the Canadian firm, the decision can be appealed to the new "binding" disputes mechanism. But the appeal can only challenge whether U.S. laws have been "faithfully and correctly" applied – the merits of the case will be argued using rules established by the U.S.

This is, to say the least, a bizarre result. I believe it is fair to say it never occurred to anyone on either side of the free trade debate that the "binding mechanism" would really validate existing practice. The least anyone expected was a new set of mutually formulated, mutually agreed, mutually accepted rules to apply. Instead, Canada has simply become a participant in maintaining a system of American protection exactly as it is.

This is the high point of Canadian achievement: the rest is downhill.

Regional development and social programs: Mulroney has claimed a great victory because regional development and social programs are not included in the agreement. There is no reason for them to be. The expectation that they would be part of a deal was based on the assumption that current U.S. trade laws would be replaced by a new set of rules. In this case Americans would insist on very stringent definitions of unfair subsidies – strict enough to have the same effect on Canadian imports as current laws have. The Canadian negotiators simply lacked the stomach to stand up against the long and aggressive U.S. list of what would be considered unfair trade practices, or to bear the heat in Canada when the concessions became

■■■■■■■■■■■■■■■■■■■■■■■■■■■■■■■■■

known. They took the easy route and just let the current laws stand.

Since there is nothing in this agreement to replace U.S. legislation, there was no need to spell out what an unfair subsidy is. The U.S. can continue to define a subsidy in virtually any way it wants and can continue to challenge our practices through their own legislative processes. It can continue to harass us over such issues as regional, provincial, and local development schemes; aspects of our unemployment insurance program; government aid to resource sectors; research and development grants; corporate tax policies; and the operation of national railroads – whenever these involve exports to the U.S. All these areas remain vulnerable to American challenge. The most we can say for Mulroney's "victory" is that it's true in a literal sense; regional development and social programs are not explicitly referred to in the agreement.

Mulroney's grand design to "secure" access to the American market has failed. Unless we "harmonize" our social and economic programs to conform to U.S. notions of what is fair play, we will have no improved access to American markets. And our social and economic programs are in greater danger than ever before. Why? Because our economy will be even more closely tied to the U.S. as a result of this agreement, and Canada will have even more to fear from U.S. complaints if our programs aren't sufficiently similar to theirs.

Energy: The free trade agreement binds us to more than just a pathetic disputes settlement mechanism. We are bound to give up what is potentially the most effective weapon we have in gaining a competitive advantage with the U.S. – our control over energy pricing and our energy supply. It is ironic that the one area where we will see "enhanced" access (as in "secure and enhance" – the government's rationale for entering into the agreement) to the U.S. market is under terms that will severely disadvantage us.

This agreement has given the U.S. something we have

███████████████████████████████████

historically resisted – total access to our energy supplies.
The gravity of the problem is indicated by the fact we
have given up our ability to reserve for Canadians our
resources even when they are very scarce. The agreement
specifically states that when energy is in short supply, the
U.S. will have "proportional access to the diminished
supply." The National Energy Board will no longer be
able to limit exports because our supply is threatened. It
will merely be able to perform a "monitoring function."

In a country as cold as ours, the ability to provide
energy at lower prices than those that competitors pay is
very important. Because of our small population, our
short growing season, and the tremendous distances here,
our production costs tend to be higher for each item made.
The abundance of energy could have provided a competitive advantage for Canadian producers. Instead, this
competitive advantage has been bargained – I use the term
loosely – away.

Services: Negotiating free trade in services is an
extraordinary concession to the U.S. on Canada's part.
Despite a massive overall trade deficit, the U.S. maintains a healthy surplus in its services account. Canada, in
contrast, has a huge trade deficit in services. So, while
we are a service economy, in that about two-thirds of our
national income derives from services and about 70 per
cent of our labour force works in service industries, we
are not a significant exporter of services. Nor are we
likely to gain major export capacities in this area in the
future. This element of the deal clearly benefits the U.S.
far more than Canada.

International trade agreements have excluded services
because of resistance from countries that see foreign
control of their service sectors as a major threat to their
control over their own economic and social programs.
The U.S., on the other hand, is desperate to negotiate
fixed rules in services so that present barriers to trade can
be removed and new ones cannot be put into place. It is
the great hope for reducing the U.S. trade deficit.

■■■■■■■■■■■■■■■■■■■■■■■■■■■■■■■

The only text now available of the elements of the U.S./ Canada free trade agreement is extremely vague about the nature of the service agreement. However, the principles of ''right of establishment'' and ''right to national treatment'' have been accepted. These are even more important for the U.S. because the selling of services across borders is less important to them than the right to set up business in services here in Canada.

However, even the enhanced right to deliver services across the border will affect Canadian jobs. This will be particularly important in industries such as computer services, data-processing, transportation, and communications. For example, there are now some restrictions on data flows across borders. If these restrictions are lifted, there could be substantial job losses in data-processing in Canada.

The ''right to national treatment'' may seriously affect the way services are delivered in Canada. With this provision, U.S. service firms in Canada will be able to challenge any Canadian practices that tend to inhibit their ability to compete here. This will pose a danger to our method of delivery, particularly when private U.S. firms compete with publicly supported services here. For example, private U.S. health-care organizations or day-care facilities may be in a position to claim equal access to public Canadian funding as a right to national treatment – peculiar as this may seem. Decisions about the public funding of private service companies will be taken out of the realm of public discussion and will be decided by trade legislation.

Manufacturing: In its defence of the agreement the government has said nothing about the impact on the manufacturing sector, except to admit that some industries may be harmed. However, removing all tariffs and import quotas will have a dramatic impact on workers in industries now protected to some degree. In the manufacturing sector these industries include textiles, clothing, food-processing, leather, footwear, furniture, petrochemicals, plastics, home appliances, and paper products.

While the government maintains that the agreement leaves the Auto Pact intact, the effect of tariff removal will be to make the safeguards of Canadian jobs in the Auto Pact ineffective. Textiles and clothing, food-processing, and auto manufacturing are the three largest industrial employers in the country and account for about one-third of Canada's industrial employment. The loss of jobs in these industries will have a major impact on the economy.

Agriculture: The free trade agreement will seriously affect Canada's ability to maintain control over our food supply. Our different conditions of production, because of our climate, have made protection essential if our agriculture is to survive. Removing tariffs and eliminating or reducing import quotas will adversely affect industries that supply the domestic market. Those most vulnerable will be farmers who produce fruit and vegetables, poultry and eggs, and dairy products. The changes in the pricing policies in the wine industry will have an immediate impact on grape growers and wine producers.

Culture: The Mulroney government maintains that the agreement permits it to retain "full capacity to support cultural industries in Canada." This is clearly untrue. The document specifically denies the government the right to support Canadian magazine publishers through lower postal rates. Differential postal rates for U.S. and Canadian publishers are considered discriminatory.

The agreement does state that cultural industries are exempt from the provisions of the agreement, but it does *not* say – despite the government's claim – that Canada retains full capacity to support its cultural industries. Thus, cultural industries still will be threatened in the ways that they have been in the past.

The definition of what constitutes a legal subsidy and which industries will be affected by this definition are still to be negotiated over the next seven years and will be included in a renegotiated disputes settlement mecha-

■■■■■■■■■■■■■■■■■■■■■■■■■■■■■■

nism. In effect, Canada is entering ongoing negotiations. But we are beginning them at a terrific disadvantage because we have given away our major bargaining issues. We will have little to influence the way the U.S. wants to define an illegal subsidy. This becomes very important when we consider what may happen in the future with cultural issues, among others. The government has tended, in the past, to give up things as a gesture of good-will, to ensure U.S. co-operation. (The drug patent bill is a good example.) The American cultural industries have long demanded greater access to the Canadian market. In negotiating a new subsidies code, it is likely that many of our present practices will be considered unfair barriers to trade. We will be back at the table with little to show and even less with which to bargain.

The politics: In his speech before Parliament defending the agreement, Prime Minister Mulroney boasted about the way his government "brings Canadians into the decision-making process." This is political doubletalk of a high order. Ordinary Canadians have not been involved in this process – it has been an initiative of big business and the Conservative government. The latest polls indicate that more people in Canada are against free trade than are for it. Before he was elected, Mulroney assured the people of this country that he was against it. He said: "Don't talk to me about free trade. That issue was decided in 1911. Free trade is a danger to Canadian sovereignty. You'll hear no more of it from me." After he was elected he changed his mind. For a while he made a show of listening to provincial leaders, but now he maintains that the provinces can have no say over the deal because it is a federal matter.

The secrecy surrounding the negotiations and the closed nature of decisions at this stage are about as undemocratic as they could possibly be. If Mulroney proceeds without taking the wishes of people into account he may precipitate a political crisis of an order not seen before in Canada.

■■■■■■■■■■■■■■■■■■■■■■■■■■■■■■

"... we should rededicate ourselves to finding our own solutions to a better economic future ..."

David Crane

David Crane is a writer on political and economic affairs for
The Toronto Star. *During his newspaper career, he has
travelled widely reporting on national and international issues
such as Canadian–U.S. relations and foreign investment
policy. He is recognized as a staunch defender of Canadian
economic independence.*

The desire by Canadians for a distinct society is real. A
June, 1987, survey on Canadian foreign policy attitudes
conducted for the Department of External Affairs by the
Longwoods Research Group found that Canadians placed
an extremely high value on their independence and control over their own affairs. Moreover, the survey showed,
Canadians want to use that independence to play an active
role in world affairs. "Canadians believe their government can have an impact in the world, even on issues that
are not specifically Canadian in their nature and origin,"
the survey report said.

■■■■■■■■■■■■■■■■■■■■■■■■■■■■■

The Longwoods survey also showed, "Canadians would like Canada to be substantially more independent from the United States than they currently perceive it as being." Two-thirds of Canadians believe "Canada should pursue its own independent policies even if this leads to certain problems in its relations with the United States," but 70 per cent of Canadians fear that what the Mulroney government is doing is to "maintain a generally close relationship with the United States even if it means certain Canadian interests have to be sacrificed." Nearly three-quarters of Canadians feel that in its dealings with the United States, Canada "does not push its own point of view strongly enough."

With the present Canada-U.S. Free Trade Agreement it is hard to see how Canada would continue to pursue its own foreign policy, for it would make itself even more dependent on the United States than it is today. As we harmonized our economic policies with the United States we would be drawn inevitably into the U.S. political and cultural orbit as well. There would be a higher risk in disagreeing with the United States and the rest of the world, even more than it does today, would see us as an echo of U.S. policies.

In 1970, with an oil crisis impending, the United States under President Richard Nixon tried to negotiate a continental energy pact with Canada that would, among other things, accelerate the development of Canadian oil reserves to meet future U.S. needs. A U.S. cabinet task force on oil, headed by then Labour Secretary George Shultz, urged negotiation of a "common energy accord" with Canada to promote "continental self-sufficiency." In a separate report, Interior Secretary Walter Hickel, Commerce Secretary Maurice Stans, and Federal Power Commission Chairman John Nassikas urged that the United States "negotiate with Canada toward a common energy policy which would provide secure supplies of oil and gas to the United States and which would cover all energy sources." Increased oil and gas imports from Can-

ada would not create balance-of-payments problems, the
U.S. officials observed. ''About one-third of the Canadian manufacturing sector is beneficially owned in the
United States so that any incremental purchases (of Canadian oil) will generate requirements for additional investment and/or greater flows of remitted profits to the
United States.'' Canada declined to negotiate a continental energy agreement at the time but after the oil shock of
1973-74, when OPEC quadrupled world prices the United
States argued that Canada should not charge it to the
world price for oil because Canada's oil reserves had been
developed by U.S.-owned companies. According to a
confidential memo from the Department of Industry,
Trade and Commerce outlining discussions with the
United States in 1970, the United States wanted to ensure
that Canadians paid the same price for oil and gas as
Americans and to ''preclude Canada from using indigenous natural gas and oil as a means of industrial development and nullify the comparative advantage we could
obtain from these resources.''

With the proposed trade agreement that has now been
negotiated, the United States achieves many of its Canadian goals. It now has a continental energy policy. The
way has been paved for increased ownership and control
of the Canadian economy by U.S. business, with even
more of our business decisions being made in the United
States. Our financial and other service industries will be
integrated with those of the United States. And Canada's
capacity to pursue its own policies in the future will be
reduced as our economy is more closely bound to that of
the United States and our policies harmonized with those
of the United States.

So instead of turning over our future to the United
States and to North American market forces, I believe we
should rededicate ourselves to finding our own solutions
to a better economic future, and with it a better quality
of life as represented by our social, cultural, and political

■■■■■■■■■■■■■■■■■■■■■■■■■■■■■■■■

achievements. And there is a choice. It is not a matter of Canada-U.S. free trade or stagnation.

Continued trade liberalization will occur through the Uruguay round of trade talks under the General Agreement on Tariffs and Trade. We will achieve lower tariffs with the United States and the rest of the world. We will get a better and more neutral system of settling trade disputes through GATT. We will get an improved code on fair and unfair subsidies. We will deal with agriculture. There will be some rules on world trade in services. GATT itself will become a stronger body to manage a world trading system. But we will do all this on a multilateral basis. Instead of a small Canada having to negotiate alone in a room with the United States, we will be at a bigger table with countries from the rest of the world where there will be more balanced bargaining. So we don't need a Canada-U.S. trade agreement to pursue trade liberalization and counter protectionism. We can get that through GATT.

But at the same time we have to do much more at home to ensure our transition to a new kind of economy based on the information revolution and high technology. We can and must do a great deal more to strengthen education and training for Canadians, to develop the human capital for the future. We can give research and development a much bigger push. We can dismantle interprovincial barriers and have free trade in Canada. We can ensure that risk capital is available to help our entrepreneurs grow and allow other industries to modernize. We can pursue the diffusion of new technology throughout our economy. We can seek better ways, based on local initiative, to solve the problems of regional disparity. And we can pursue policies to build up strong Canadian-owned companies and to assist them in finding the growing markets of Asia, Europe, and Latin America, as well as the United States. Given the chance, Canadian companies can compete.

We can create the wealth to continue the Canadian experiment in nation-building and play a bigger role in world affairs. We don't need such a free trade agreement. Like our ancestors in 1911 we should say "no." But in saying "no" we must also work hard to pursue the alternative, independent direction for Canada. We can do it.

While it is true that Canada-U.S. free trade can mean lower prices for consumers, there is more to life than shopping. Canadians have always been willing to pay a price to pursue their own public philosophy, one that is the basis for medicare, regional development, crown corporations, environmental safeguards, clean and well-planned cities, cultural institutions such as the CBC, equalization payments, and other policies and regulations that help to define our country. And this is clearly at risk in a free trade pact.

■■■■■■■■■■■■■■■■■■■■■■■■■■■■
". . . free trade will open Canada to more American images, ideas, and sentiments than we ever thought possible."

Jerry Goodis

Jerry Goodis, a pioneer in Canada's advertising industry, is president of Jerry Goodis Inc., one of the nation's major advertising agencies. He is also the author of Have I Ever Lied To You Before?

Free. It is a word we all know. In my thirty years in advertising and marketing, I have become especially familiar with it. Like most people, though, I view the word with healthy suspicion. That is because very few things are free. Look behind a great deal, and you will find hidden costs. This is my objection to our so-called free trade agreement with the United States. It is a deal that is destined to exact intolerable prices from my profession and, ultimately, from Canada itself. It is, in short, the most expensive bargain we have ever considered.

Mine is a business of ideas. And I think good ideas are good ideas, no matter where they start. American jazz,

104

■■■■■■■■■■■■■■■■■■■■■■■■■■■■■■■

Canadian hockey, and Italian food have fans throughout the world. What is more, a nation's willingness to accept new ideas is really a mark of its strength and security. The problem comes when a younger culture is forced to receive ideas that are antithetical to its traditions. In terms of advertising alone, free trade will open Canada to more American images, ideas, and sentiments than we ever thought possible.

We in Canada have strong cultural values and traditions. We are getting over our sheepishness about them. And those who wish to persuade us through advertising know they must consider these traditions if their work is to succeed. But at least two of our strongest traditions are at distinct odds with the American experience. One is our relative acceptance of diversity. We take pride in our multicultural society, and we are loath to impose any standard of sameness on newcomers.

The other tradition involves our historical ties with both the French and English languages. This latter tradition is generally well respected by Canadian advertisers. That is because success in Canada's French market depends on a very precise adaptation of marketing strategy. Simply translating English ads word-for-word does not work, and plenty of my colleagues have the battle scars to prove it.

My fear is that free trade will give American communicators new ways to reach us with slanted messages that are totally unsuited to our culture. My fear, too, is that this new American stranglehold on advertising will mean the end of the Canadian industry as we now know it. This fear is becoming a reality even now. Many of Canada's largest ad agencies are actually branches of international firms based in New York. I have observed that some of these agencies view Canada as just another segment of the vast U.S. market. Free trade promises to turn their fantasy into fact.

It will happen because American communicators benefit from economies of scale that could never exist here. If an American is printing 15 million catalogues or brochures or direct-mail pieces, for example, the cost of printing a few million more to cover Canada will be modest. So modest, in fact, that Canadian printers will be hard pressed to stay in business. The same principle will apply to television production: why produce a commercial just for Canada when, for a fraction of the cost, you can use one cranked out by a non-union crew in the States? Ultimately, it is a question that should strike fear in the heart of every Canadian who is in this business. The American market is roughly ten times the size of ours. Since American agencies can therefore create marketing strategies with greater cost efficiency, this country's ad shops are doomed to redundancy – as are all their suppliers, including typesetters, printers, writers, artists, photographers, translators, actors, production staff, and technicians, to name a few.

These people are special. I believe they are, and so do my American counterparts who have been fortunate enough to woo them away. Invariably, they tell me that Canadians bring with them a freshness, insight, and openness that delights them. And, in all modesty, I think the virtues of our expatriates are due, in large part, to the traditions of their homeland. Under free trade, these talented people will lose the luxury of choice about working in the States. If the only jobs going are in the U.S., that is where they must be. And if gifted Canadians are forced to emigrate, our country's remarkable pool of talent will soon dry up. Canada and the United States will be one, and both will be the worse for it.

Of course, there is a measure of self-interest in my concern. I want to stay in business, and I would not mind having a few Canadian competitors, either. So, yes, I am frightened. But I am frightened even more for Canada itself.

So much of American culture reflects a society that is violent and self-important. So many of its images attest to the consensus that helping the poor is a radical idea.

■■■■■■■■■■■■■■■■■■■■■■■■■■■■■■■

So much of its rhetoric supports the notion that countries seeking autonomy would do well to check with Washington first. Free trade will open new avenues for these beliefs – beliefs which, in my opinion, are an assault on the values that built our country. And there is no point in hoping that these incoming ideas will be tailored to suit our temperament. Not a chance. We will get them in all their spurious glory, because what is good for Miami will be good for Moncton, too.

I have learned this terrifying lesson in boardrooms from New York to Chicago, from Danbury to Battle Creek. In each of these cities, I have been told that I no longer had an account because the client's parent company believed an American agency could handle all of North America with greater efficiency. On these occasions, I have argued that Canada is a distinct market requiring great sensitivity to issues of language, region, and culture. I have wasted my breath, because the reply has always been that language, region, and culture have never been impediments to the company's vast international sales.

Yes, I have been there, and I have fumed at the idea that my country is a blip on a sales chart, and an insignificant blip at that. The very notion has outraged me, and outrage does not come easily to a populace that is normally so controlled and polite.

Advertising does not change the world. If it could, all the churches would be full and all the jails empty. But advertising does bring each culture reassuring or provocative reflections of its values. Every good advertiser is aware of this fact. Indeed, if anything has changed about my business in the past three decades, it is that its practitioners have become more sensitive to the ways in which their ideas mirror and influence their culture. Unfortunately, though, American marketers continue to be cheerfully oblivious to the qualities that make us different. If general communication originates in the hands and minds of non-Canadians, it will eventually change

107

us. We may resist the onslaught for a time, but it will one day take hold, distort our identity, and, finally, swamp our culture.

In a way, I can understand the allure of free trade. Duty-free shopping is fun, and Americans are friendly people. Indeed, they are so friendly, they will assure us that our concerns over free trade are unfounded. And they will mean it when they say it. But the day will come when they view us with the desire common to entrepreneurs and conquerors alike. They will plunder hundreds of professions, including my own, and not be satisfied until the territory is indisputably theirs.

The time to stop the plunder is before it begins. The time to expose free trade for all its shoddy charms is now. It is not hard to admire the power of the eagle in flight. The trick is to avoid its talons. Free trade will only make them sharper.

■■■■■■■■■■■■■■■■■■■■■■■■■■■

"It is not un-Canadian, protectionist, or timid to insist that we should fully debate such a fundamental change . . ."

Jon K. Grant

Jon. K. Grant is president and chief executive officer of the Peterborough, Ontario, based Quaker Oats Company of Canada Ltd. He sits on the board of numerous corporations and has spoken widely on issues facing the food industry.

Canada's proposed free trade agreement with the United States is essentially about natural resources, primarily energy and, perhaps, water. Obviously, both sides attached substantially different priorities and opposing objectives to this agreement.

For the Canadian government, the impetus to finalize a free trade agreement with the United States developed so quickly in Ottawa that it was never part of a federal election campaign: in fact, all parties leading up to the last election opposed the idea. Concern about American protectionism, however, moved Ottawa to seek to guarantee our continued access to American markets.

■■■■■■■■■■■■■■■■■■■■■■■■■■■■■■■■■■■

From the Americans' point of view there were certainly not the same factors operating in their country in the direction of an agreement. For them it was a real opportunity to rationalize North American energy resources and to achieve a long-term continental deal in sharing hydrocarbon and hydroelectric energy – and possibly water resources as well. The energy card may have been played too early in the game, and in the remainder of the negotiations we had lost our leverage to strengthen other elements of the deal.

Because free trade was not an issue in the election of only three years ago, Canadians must now have the opportunity of thoroughly and openly questioning the gains and losses of a continental free trade arrangement. It is not un-Canadian, protectionist, or timid to insist that we should fully debate such a fundamental change in our Canadian social and economic system. Without the vehicle of an election, Canadians of every shade of opinion should still insist on their right to enter into a comprehensive national referendum. As a Canadian with some knowledge of agriculture, I would welcome such a discussion.

In the case of our farm population and its allied interests, there has been a significant lack of awareness, concern, and information on the economic fate of the Canadian farmer in a free trade Canada. Canada has a northern climate with a small and widely distributed population. Agricultural costs, possibly excepting the case of beef cattle and our world-class wheat, have always been higher than those of the United States. Longer American growing seasons have contributed to substantial efficiencies.

At present, with the discounted Canadian dollar and with tariff rates on American foodstuffs ranging from 5 to 17.5 per cent, our two systems are essentially in balance. Even then, in the last five years our importation of processed food products from the United States has been climbing steadily. In Ontario alone, the leading food-

111

manufacturing province, about 10 per cent of the province's manufacturing labour force is employed in the
manufacture of agricultural commodities. Eighty per cent
of Ontario farm production is absorbed in food processing. The elimination of tariffs on processed foods over
the next ten years could substantially destabilize our agricultural industry, particularly in mixed farming.

Ironically, agricultural stabilization programs and supply management marketing boards have been excluded
from the terms of a free trade agreement. With the competitive impact of lower-priced raw food and processed
products from the United States in our markets, however,
we face the danger that price and supply mechanisms will
be forced out of existence. It is arguable that these mechanisms may now provide unneeded protection for certain
sectors of our farming community, but that is a marginal
consideration. On most Canadian farms today, one or
more members of the family must earn ''off-farm''
income to augment their reduced farm returns. By every
measure – farm living standards, return on investment,
and return on assets – average farm incomes are already
lower than those of comparable urban families.

For the food processor, moreover, whether the company is a multinational or Canadian-owned, the dismantling of tariff barriers will force either raw materials or
finished processed products to originate from the lower-
cost supply point.

Under a north-south trading agreement, Canadian food
processors may find themselves at the end of a rail line
that no longer runs east-west. A food-processing plant in
Kentucky or Kansas could much more easily draw raw
materials from the large farm belt in the continent's more
temperate regions. Then, following a shipping pattern
like spokes in a wheel from that geographic centre, it
would distribute to its customers, including, ultimately,
the Canadians.

Food processors in Canada, faced with reducing their
own prices by 10 per cent in order to compete with tariff-

■■■■■■■■■■■■■■■■■■■■■■■■■■■■■

free American imports, would put substantial pressure on Canadian farm-gate prices. Farm rationalization would then follow inevitably, with some farm commodities phased out as rural populations and agricultural land prices decline.

A recent Goldfarb survey indicated that farmers are respected more than any other institutional group: 75 per cent for farmers; 50 per cent for bankers. The farm family is still a reality for many Canadians who are tied to land, and a continuing symbol of stability for many others. The political implication of destabilizing Canadian agriculture at a time when worldwide commodity prices are low holds major risks for any government: politicians earned 31 per cent in the Goldfarb survey.

Even without free trade, some farm rationalization in Canada is occurring by natural processes; marketing boards may also lose some of their power to fix prices and to control supply. An arbitrary acceleration of those processes, however, without carefully planned social adjustments, could mean abandoned farms, ghost towns and villages, and a reduced rural base. To many of us for whom the farm is still reality or a significant symbol, such an accelerated decline offers a depressing prospect.

The food business employs 230,000 Canadians, and it is a $40 billion industry, exceeded only by petroleum and automobile manufacturing. With so much of our attention in the free trade discussion centred on energy and the manufacture of automobiles, it is disturbing that there has been so little concern for the future of Canada's food supply and food industry. As Canadians, we have every right to debate and to judge who the free trade winners and losers will be. It is, emphatically, not unpatriotic to do so. Economic decisions must be balanced by social consequences. That is in the Canadian tradition.

114

■■■■■■■■■■■■■■■■■■■■■■■■■■■■

"Every time we negotiate with the Americans we lose our shirts."

Harold Horwood

Harold Horwood is Newfoundland's best-known writer. He was a member of the team headed by Joey Smallwood that brought Newfoundland into Confederation. He was subsequently elected to the Newfoundland legislature for the District of Labrador.

Every time we negotiate with the Americans we lose our shirts. One hundred and fifty years ago, after we had beaten them in the War of 1812, after we had thrown their armies out of Canada, after the Nova Scotia privateers had put an end to their Atlantic trade, and we were occupying half of what's now the state of Maine, we sat down to negotiate a peace treaty in which we not only gave it all back to them but gave them a chunk of Canada in the bargain, including what's now the city of Detroit.

After the so-called Aroostook War, actually a dispute between loggers on the upper reaches of the St. John

River when the Americans called out a militia to enforce their claim to our waterways, we again sat down to negotiate with them. And lo and behold, they walked away with a large chunk of New Brunswick, which they gleefully added to the state of Maine!

Everyone knows what happened when we negotiated with them over the boundaries of Alaska and the state of Washington. They talked us out of hundreds of miles of the British Columbia coastline, now known as the Alaska Panhandle, as well as a slice of the British Columbia lower mainland; thus they moved a long way toward achieving their ambition to cut Canada off from the Pacific Ocean entirely.

Even when they talk ''free trade'' what they really mean is annexation – Manifest Destiny – their presumed right to rule the whole North American continent. This was never shown more clearly than in the three attempts by Newfoundland to negotiate a free trade deal with the Americans in the half century or so before Newfoundland entered the Canadian union in 1949.

The Americans had always claimed rights in Newfoundland waters, including fishing rights dating back to the time when the original thirteen states were thirteen British colonies, and Newfoundland repeatedly tried to get a compensating right to land fish duty free in the United States. The Washington Treaty of 1888 between Canada, Newfoundland, and the United States was designed to guarantee such American rights on our fishing grounds and to give us a measure of free trade in return. The treaty was never ratified by Congress. Instead, the Americans enjoyed the benefits of the treaty for two years, while continuing to restrict Canadian and Newfoundland imports, and then repudiated the treaty altogether, an action described by Canadian historians as ''dishonourable.''

Newfoundland next tried to go it alone, without Canadian support, and succeeded in negotiating the Bond-Blaine Treaty of 1890, chief negotiators being Robert

Bond of Newfoundland and James Blaine, the American Secretary of State. Again, Newfoundland was to get preferred tariff treatment in exchange for fishing rights, and cured fish (though not fresh fish) was to enter the American market duty free.

The Americans saw this modest deal as a step toward statehood by Newfoundland and tried to use that as an argument to quiet the objections of the New England fishing corporations, who wanted to catch Newfoundland fish themselves, and buy and use Newfoundland bait, but yearned to enjoy the benefits of protective tariffs at the same time. The American press, with Boston alone dissenting, hailed the Bond-Blaine Treaty as a step in the process of Manifest Destiny. "Newfoundland moves toward statehood," the papers announced.

Canada objected to a deal that did not include the Maritimes and the treaty was never ratified. The British tried to convince Newfoundland that she should join the Canadian union instead, but Newfoundlanders, blaming Canada for the failure of the treaty, erected a fence of protective measures, including measures directed at both Canada and the United States. Bond tried again in 1902, his opposite number this time being Secretary of State John Hay. They reached an agreement similar to that of 1890, but Senator Henry Cabot Lodge, representing the New England fishing interests, managed to insert so many amendments into the bill, imposing so many restrictions on the Newfoundland trade, that the Newfoundlanders broke off the attempt to get the treaty ratified.

Finally, in 1947 a group of young men at St. John's formed the Economic Union with the United States Party and secured the backing of a large majority of the United States Senate. However, it became perfectly clear that what the Americans wanted was not free trade but another state on their northeastern border, a state that would be one more move toward the encirclement and eventual absorption of Canada.

They managed to find a few Newfoundlanders to come

117

out publicly with the statement that what they really wanted was not just economic union but annexation of their country by the Americans, and Colonel Bertie McCormick, publisher of the *Chicago Tribune*, began a newspaper campaign with that end in view. "Newfoundland soon to be 49th State?" his headline asked and his protégée in the government, Senator Brooks, issued a long statement on closer economic ties as a step closer to statehood.

In 1948 Newfoundlanders voted instead to become a province of Canada. But Manifest Destiny has never died in the United States. By the 1980s the Americans had found a new champion, a smooth-talking Canadian politician. He, too, believed in Manifest Destiny.

Canadians, a mild-mannered and unsuspicious people, accepted Brian Mulroney at face value and elected him to be their Prime Minister by a majority of the popular vote, never suspecting that he was an American puppet, dancing on the strings of American expansionism. When his government began negotiating with the United States for what they called a free trade deal, the people of Canada assumed that Canada's vital interests would be protected or no deal would be signed. Only very gradually did it become apparent that Mulroney and his government were prepared to go to any lengths to get some kind of a deal, any kind of a deal, no matter how one-sided it might be, no matter how favourable it might be to the Americans, no matter how damaging to Canada. If "freer trade," as the government continued to call it, should start an inevitable slide toward the political absorption of Canada by the Americans, what was wrong with that? Wouldn't we be better off if the Americans took us over politically, as well as economically?

Canadians, meanwhile, have repudiated Mulroney by a vast majority. It has reached the point where little more than one-fifth of the voters in the country support him. But that makes no difference. He plunges straight ahead, determined to push the country into the American law during his one term in office. He'll be defeated, of course, in the next election. But by then his mission will be accomplished.

And that's where we stand today: a repudiated Prime Minister insisting on concluding a dangerous and even disastrous treaty with a foreign country that has never shown a willingness to treat us as an equal, but only an eagerness to swallow us up.

In all decency, the so-called free trade agreement should be placed squarely before the people of Canada, all its provisions spelled out and explained, and we should have the chance to vote for or against it, either in a plebiscite or in a general election. We should not be committed behind our backs to giving up our economic independence, or what's left of it, our cultural independence, or what little we ever had, and our political independence, which we fought and worked so hard to secure.

■ ■

"... never in our very worst dreams did we imagine that a government of Canada would ever give away so much for so little gain."

Mel Hurtig

Mel Hurtig is the president of Hurtig Publishers and the creator of The Canadian Encyclopedia. *He is the founder and honorary chairman of the Council of Canadians, a public interest group concerned with matters relating to Canada's economic, political, and cultural sovereignty. Mel Hurtig lives in Edmonton.*

From 1978 to 1985, inclusive, Canadian-controlled companies in Canada increased employment by 876,200 jobs; U.S.-controlled companies increased employment by only 1,400 jobs. Canadian-controlled companies increased employment by over 16 per cent; U.S.-controlled companies increased employment by 0.1 per cent. In the goods-producing sector of the Canadian economy, Canadian-controlled companies increased employment by 102,600 jobs, while U.S.-controlled companies *decreased* employment by 61,000 jobs.

In the period 1978–1984 (1985 figures are not yet avail-

■■■■■■■■■■■■■■■■■■■■■■■■■■■■■■■■■■

able), Canadian-controlled companies, for every billion dollars in profits, created 5,765 new jobs. During the same period, for every billion dollars in profits earned, U.S.-controlled companies created seventeen jobs! Put another way, U.S. firms took one-third of all profits, yet created only one-tenth of one per cent of new jobs.

During this same period of time the profits of U.S.-controlled companies in Canada more than doubled, from $8.3 billion in 1978 to $16.9 billion in 1984. For *all* foreign-controlled companies in Canada, profits doubled from $9.9 billion to $19.8 billion, while employment actually *decreased* by 12,800 jobs!

Small Canadian-owned companies with fewer than twenty employees created 819,600 new jobs during this period, or over 93.5 per cent of all new jobs. At the same time, large Canadian firms, with over 100 employees, actually *reduced* the number of jobs by 31,900. It is precisely these same large firms (along with U.S. multinational corporations) that are the chief proponents of the ''free'' trade agreement with the U.S. (Most of the small Canadian firms were *not* engaged in significant export activities.) Perhaps the most shocking figures are to be found in the goods-producing sector. Small Canadian-controlled firms increased employment by 220,600 jobs while the large Canadian-controlled firms *decreased* employment by 189,500 jobs.

It is beyond my comprehension how any group of Canadian citizens could have agreed to the horrendously bad deal that is the free trade agreement. Those of us who were concerned three years ago, when the first leaks surfaced about the government's intentions to negotiate such a deal, were very apprehensive. But never in our very worst dreams did we imagine that a government of Canada would ever give away so much for so little gain.

There will be no Canada within a generation if the Mulroney government is allowed to proceed with its plans. The massive abandonment of sovereignty, the increased integration, the inevitable harmonization, the increased

122

■■■■■■■■■■■■■■■■■■■■■■■■■■■■■■

dependency and vulnerability, the increased American
ownership and control of our industry and resources, and
the certain severe economic consequences will combine
to put an end forever to the dream of Canada. Perhaps
the country will not formally disappear in our lifetimes,
but the result will be, at best, a colony or trust territory
without any ability to control its future. More likely, the
same people who are now advocating this unprecedented
"leap of faith" will then set out to convince Canadians
they have no alternative but to appeal to Americans for
political union. "After all, if all the key decisions about
our future are made in Washington, hadn't we better have
some senators down there, and some members in the
House of Representatives?"

This "trade agreement" is a massive abandonment of
Canadian sovereignty. If implemented it will be irrever-
sible. We will be saying that once and for all we are giving
up on the idea of Canada.

■■■■■■■■■■■■■■■■■■■■■■■■■■■■■
"... marching backward into

the future."

George Ignatieff

George Ignatieff has had a distinguished career in Canada's foreign service, including serving as High Commissioner to the U.K. and ambassador to the United Nations. Ignatieff served as a negotiator at GATT. In 1980, he became Chancellor of the University of Toronto. He is also president of the organization Science for Peace.

As a former negotiator on trade for Canada at GATT, I am keenly aware that it is the fine print that is important if we are to judge the advantages and disadvantages of the free trade agreement. What we know so far, however, leads me to believe that the main objective of GATT – management of trade on a global basis – is not recognized by the Reagan-Mulroney initiative.

What we have here is continentalist and is addressed primarily to American trading interests. The machinery for settling disputes, for instance, is to be based on American trade laws, not GATT rules. Furthermore, as

The New York Times pointed out the day after the free trade agreement was initialled, the Canada-United States accord was ''paving the way for greater competition in an *integrated* North American market.'' Today Canada; tomorrow the world.

The European Economic Community has already noted the potential harm arising from this continentalist approach. ''It's worrying for us,'' an EEC official stated in early October, ''if the U.S. pulls back from global trade into some regional inward-looking block as it pushes ahead ruthlessly to demand international trade rules on its own terms.''

The abolition of tariffs is not the challenge and the danger of the free trade agreement; rather, the danger lies in the actual new political message the agreement gives to the world: the United States has become the leader of a new economic bloc. Will it not work out its ''manifest destiny'' at the exclusion of any other interests, including Canada's?

In a world of growing interdependence in trade, what Canada should be seeking is global – and not continental – co-operation. GATT is a good instrument in this regard, for it offers a global approach more compatible with world interdependence, resulting from the network of world communications and the increasing global fluidity of world commerce and finance. The conservative leaders of the U.S.A. and Canada seem to be marching backward into the future.

"We have done the

unthinkable."

Martin Katz

Martin Katz is a graduate of the Faculties of Law of the University of Toronto and of the Université de Paris I. He has been a Professor of Labour Law and Business Law at the Université de Moncton and has written on international trade law.

Just before midnight on October 3, 1987, Canada and the U.S.A. initialled the Canada-U.S. Free Trade Agreement (FTA) in Washington, D.C. The FTA establishes a free trade area between Canada and the U.S.A. The two sovereign nations have agreed to allow money to cross the border relatively free of government intervention. Thus, trade in goods, trade in services, and investment are intended to occur in a North American context.

Under the agreement, industry will be free to seek elements of production of the lowest cost, whether in the U.S.A. or Canada. Cheaper goods and labour to business mean cheaper products to consumers.

126

■■■■■■■■■■■■■■■■■■■■■■■■■■■■■■■■

The tab for these imported goods and services will be paid by those sectors of Canadian industry that will lose sales or jobs to the cheaper producers in other countries. Those lost sales will mean the closing down of some suppliers in Canada and the dislocation of owners and workers in the affected industries. The cheaper imported goods have two prices – the direct cost on the price tag and the hidden or indirect cost of social dislocation, including bankruptcy, UIC cheques, violence, unhappiness, and other fall-out generally linked to unemployment.

Every country in the world erects barriers to trade in the form of tariffs and non-tariffs (including subsidies). These barriers are not intended to bring harm to other countries. Rather, they are intended to raise the cost to industry of buying goods outside the country, thus encouraging the purchase of goods with a higher price tag within the country and avoiding some of the hidden social cost associated with international competition. It is difficult to quantify the advantages of social well-being regarding everything from health and safety and pollution standards to bilingual packaging and metric measurements, from non-discriminatory employment requirements to minimum-wage legislation, and to appreciate them in the face of higher price tags on some consumer durables, but that is the trade-off that must be borne in mind when judging the desirability of free trade.

Regardless of the effect on the prices of North American-made consumer durables, the free trade agreement will alter fundamentally, dramatically, and irreversibly the way Canadians live from day to day. This thesis can be analysed by looking at the agreement provisions regarding cultural industries and standards harmonization.

Cultural Industries

In general, the free trade agreement addresses the concerns of Canadian cultural nationalists by exempting ''cultural industries'' from its provisions. The agreement defines a cultural industry as an enterprise engaged in any

127

of five categories of activity: traditional publishing, film and video production, musical recordings, music videos, and radio/television. The effect of this exemption is disastrous. It defines culture for Canadians. Culture is limited to those industries named in the definition. Any activity other than these is not culture and is *ipso facto* business and therefore open to uninhibited, unprotected, unregulated competition from or acquisition by American industry.

We have done the unthinkable. We have, with this exemption, adopted implicitly the paradigmatic American world view that every enterprise of society is economic, existing only to produce profit, and therefore properly to be exposed to the rigours of the marketplace. From this universe, we have hived off five undertakings we acknowledge might exist for reasons additional to or other than material gain – and we have christened these five things ''Culture.''

Canada has irrevocably denied, by signing an international treaty including this exemption clause, that Canadian culture is actually a collective mindset constituted by and including such phenomena as: federally regulated banks; publicly funded egalitarian universities; publicly funded, non-military scientific research; stabilizing, centrally planned agricultural boards; meaningful mandatory automobile insurance; strict firearm regulation; strict environmental protection legislation; paternalistic health and safety legislation and administration; historically motivated regional support and transfer payments; the Trans-Canada highway; bilingualism; multiculturalism; centro-regional tension; five-and-a-half time zones; snow. We have denied that when Maritime fishermen are forced to be more efficiently productive in a factory in southern Ontario, their culture is gravely affected.

Canada has acquiesced to the American vision of culture as industry. After the free trade agreement, everything our society does is industry. While five industries

128

■■■■■■■■■■■■■■■■■■■■■■■■■■■■■■

may receive subsidies, the agreement clearly provides that a country may retaliate against any subsidy to a "cultural industry" that distorts free trade. Thus, American agreement to allow us to subsidize our "cultural industries" was obtained at a considerable cost; we agree that should a subsidy disadvantage one of their "entertainment industries," it may trigger a retaliatory duty.

Direct effects will also be felt by particular enterprises. Periodicals published in Canada will lose the benefit of a preferential postal rate that represents a savings of hundreds of thousands of dollars and allows many periodicals (of Canadians, by Canadians) to exist in a market dominated by inexpensive run-on copies of American periodicals. Broadcasters and cable companies will no longer be entitled to pirate transborder signals with impunity. Culture is on the table: it is the Blue Plate Special.

Standards Harmonization

One of the most important ways in which government has participated in the Canadian marketplace is to set standards to regulate the production of goods in order to protect health and safety, the environment, and consumer interests. The Consumer Protection Act, labour legislation relating to workplace health and safety, and environmental protection legislation all contribute to a particular manner of living in Canada. Canadians have come to expect that the profit motive will be curbed in certain circumstances in which other values (minimizing misleading or near-fraudulent sales to consumers, protecting health and safety over speed in production and manufacturing, protecting the environment) are deemed to be more important. The free trade agreement addresses such standards and jeopardizes our chances to continue to enjoy the benefits of such protective legislation.

Further, Canada and the U.S.A. agree "to harmonize federal standardsrelated [*sic*] measures to the greatest extent possible, and to promote harmonization of private

■■■■■■■■■■■■■■■■■■■■■■■■■■■■■■■■■■

standards.'' Thus, we are in the position of consulting with and setting standards together with the U.S.A. in future. Given the relative sizes of our production and markets, it is possible to foresee that our more exigent standards will be eroded downward to ''harmonize'' with more market-friendly standards of the U.S.A. There is no reason to suspect that the metric system, for example, an industrial standard that raises the cost to American industry of trading into Canada, will not fall prey to North American standards harmonization.

In a similar vein, the parties have agreed to minimize technical barriers on agriculture, food, and beverage goods. Our regulation of food contents, labelling, and packaging raises the cost to Americans of doing business across the border and thus constitutes a barrier to trade. We have by this provision agreed to co-operate with American regulatory authorities to reduce technical differences that ''interfere with trade.'' Higher costs will have to be justified by showing the necessity of a particular requirement to the protection of ''human, animal and plant health.'' Bilingual packaging can be regarded as a technical requirement which, arguably, constitutes a barrier to trade. It is not saved by the cultural industries exemption and is not likely to be considered necessary to the protection of health.

In identifying the Canadian economy with that of the U.S.A., the free trade agreement will force Canadians increasingly to act like Americans, at least in our socio-economic relations. The benefits to Canadians are unclear, at best. The upheaval the agreement will work on the way we live in Canada is astonishing in scope. Through the exercise of the federal treaty-making power, the Mulroney administration may have succeeded in fulfilling the neo-conservative dream for Canada by ensuring a tighter reign on public-sector industrial strategic planning and the domination of the free market ethic and of American-style utilitarian consumer-capitalism in Canada. It is impossible to imagine such profound inter-

■■■■■■■■■■■■■■■■■■■■■■■■■■■

ventionism in our free and democratic society without a
clear and convincing mandate. We must demand that an
election be held before the free trade agreement becomes
law. Canadians have been delivered a costly lunch. We
still have time to send it back to the kitchen before the
tab arrives; we need not accept what we did not order.

■■■■■■■■■■■■■■■■■■■■■■■■■■■
"The rules that emerge

will be rules that suit the

Americans . . ."

James Laxer

James Laxer is a writer and broadcaster of great political insight. His recent National Film Board seven-part series, "Reckoning," is a brilliant investigation of the Canadian economy. He is the author of Leap of Faith: Free Trade and the Future of Canada *and* Decline of the Superpowers: Winners and Losers in Today's Global Economy.

The Mulroney government is presenting Canadians with a shimmering vision of the benefits that are to flow from the implementation of the trade agreement they have initialled with the United States. The benefits are to be of three kinds: more jobs for Canadians; greater security of access to the American market for Canadian businesses; and lower prices for Canadian consumers.

Everyone has read the prediction that hundreds of thousands of jobs will be created in Canada when the trade agreement is implemented. The idea is a simple one and has obvious appeal. If there are no restraints on what

Canadians can export to the United States, Canadian business can be expected to make investments based on the assumption of complete access to a continental market of 275 million people, instead of having secure access to a market of only 25 million people. At last, Canadian producers will be able to avail themselves of the full benefits of economies of scale. Using the continental market to attain international competitiveness, they will later be able to go after exports anywhere in the world.

The assumption that hundreds of thousands of jobs will be created in Canada rests entirely on this logic turning out to be correct. In fact, the expectation of an employment bonanza is based on two key errors: first, that Canadian access to the American market will be significantly improved through the trade deal; and second, that in the future the American economy will continue functioning much as it has over the past five years.

Security of access to the American market has been the key goal of the Mulroney government from the beginning. When they signed the deal, the government told Canadians that the objective had been met. In fact, it had not. For the past several years, supporters of a trade deal with Washington have been pointing to the threat American trade law poses to Canadian exports to the United States. After the deal, as now, however, American trade law will remain in place. Its power to strike back at Canadian exports through the imposition of countervailing duties will continue. The basis for the claim that things have changed is that the deal involves the creation of a tribunal to be made up of Americans and Canadians to consider appeals in cases where people believe that trade law has been unfairly applied.

What this means is that a Canadian company exporting lumber, potash, or whatever could have a countervailing duty slapped on its product because it has been found guilty of unfair trading practices or has been judged to be damaging an American industry through its exports. After the countervailing duty has been levied, an appeal

134

■■■■■■■■■■■■■■■■■■■■■■■■■■■■■■■

could be made to the new tribunal. The tribunal, however, can only determine whether or not the Americans have fairly applied their own trade law. For those who have studied American trade law, this is something of a cruel joke. The relevant American trade acts have been drafted to make them as broad as possible, precisely so they can be used as a political club. Simply putting Canadians on the review tribunal will not much change the results.

A few days after the free trade agreement was signed in Washington, the U.S. trade representative's summary of the agreement was released. It contained this version of the scope in which the tribunal would work: "Accordingly, in the United States, decisions of the Commerce Department and the ITC can be overturned only if they are unsupported by substantial evidence in the administrative record, arbitrary and capricious, or otherwise not in accordance with U.S. law." The American summary makes clear that the tribunal is to have only the tiniest scope in its operations. Only in cases where the Americans have applied their own law in the most reckless fashion would the tribunal be empowered to overturn an American decision.

In defence of the tribunal, government officials point to the fact that over the next five to seven years it is to draft a new set of rules, to define the scope of fair trade practices. Are they serious? It took enormous concessions on Canada's part to move the Americans this far. In several years, once the Canadian economy is even more integrated with that of the United States, there will be no turning back. The rules that will emerge will be rules that suit the Americans or there simply will never be a set of new rules at all.

Canadians are being told that security of access to the American market will be dramatically improved as a result of the trade agreement. The claim is false. To expect huge new investments to be made in Canada based on the security gained from the creation of the tribunal is to bet on the highly improbable.

135

■■■■■■■■■■■■■■■■■■■■■■■■■■■■■■■■■■■

There is another and even more important reason not to make such a bet. The critical assumption that the American economy will continue to function much as it has over the past five years is almost certainly wrong. Since 1982, the United States has been the world's greatest importer. Its economic growth has been based not on improved production but on increased American consumption. And that increased consumption has been financed by American borrowing from foreigners. Over the past five years, the United States has become the largest net debtor nation in the world. The American economy is awash in a sea of red ink: the huge American trade deficit, the U.S. budget deficit, and the massive personal indebtedness of American citizens.

Canada's economic growth over the past five years has depended heavily on rising exports to the United States. Now, though, there are unmistakable signs that a change is coming. On Black Monday, October 19, 1987, investors rumbled out their warning as the markets of the world plunged. The crash had its immediate causes, but few serious observers doubted that the central long-term cause was the unreality of American economic policy. Over the next few years, the United States will be forced to begin living within its means. And that will result in much lower trade surpluses for the countries that are America's major trading partners, including Canada.

To believe that the trade surpluses of the last five years can go on forever is a serious mistake. The free trade agreement prepares us for the last war, not for the one we are about to fight, much like the French Maginot Line on the eve of World War II. Instead of dreaming of the creation of hundreds of thousands of jobs through additional exports that will not materialize, we should be worried about the loss of thousands of jobs in this country as Canadian tariffs come off. Assuming that a recession does take place in the global economy in the next couple of years (now a commonplace assumption), Canadians will face the closing of large numbers of American subsidiaries in this country as their owners decide to supply their Canadian markets from production facilities on the other side of the border. The jobs bonanza that is to come from free trade lies somewhere over the rainbow. Don't count on it materializing in the real world in which we live.

What about the other hope of the free-traders, that Canadians will be able to head south and fill their cars with low-priced goods and then return home facing no hassle from customs? During the ten-year period while Canadian tariffs are being phased out, duty will still have to be paid at the border on many items. In addition, it is likely that Canadians will pay federal sales taxes at the border on imported products.

The real price benefit of free trade would not come from junkets to the States to bring back the goodies, but from the availability of cheaper products in the stores in Canada. Of all the claims of the free-traders, this one is the most plausible. Greater access to the Canadian market for U.S. producers should bring our prices down closer to American levels. In calculating this benefit, however, don't forget three things: the exchange rate on the Canadian dollar will still make the Canadian price tag higher than the American price tag; prices in Canada will tend not to fall all the way to the American level as car buyers in this country have known well in the twenty-two years since the Auto Pact went into effect; and, most important, additional U.S. imports occur at the expense of Canadian jobs. Few people would trade their jobs for slightly lower prices, and few others would want to pay unemployment and welfare benefits to support those who are laid off.

I can only conclude that when government ministers signed the deal, their minds were focused on the vision of a theoretically beautiful free trade agreement. Let us hope the hallucination will end and that they will wake up to the actual deal they have signed.

■■■■■■■■■■■■■■■■■■■■■■■■■■■■■■

"... it's the acceptance of inequality that I fear most."

Jack Layton

Jack Layton is a Toronto alderman and a member of Toronto's Metro and City councils. He is also chair of the Board of Health for Toronto and is visiting professor in the faculty of Environmental Studies at York University, teaching courses in local government and planning.

When I first read the news about Miami – an American city popular with some Canadians – that now anyone would be able to carry a handgun legally, I had two reactions. I decided that I would not be going to Miami again. (I had never felt particularly comfortable there anyway.) Then, thankful, I jumped to the comfortable conclusion that it could never happen here, in our Canadian cities.

But could it? They tell us free trade will let us be more like them. Won't our cities, therefore, be more like theirs? The logic seems too dangerously obvious to be ignored or discounted. Free trade, as others have pow-

■■■■■■■■■■■■■■■■■■■■■■■■■■■■■■

erfully shown, will speed the integration of our economies. But "economies" are, essentially, ways of living. So in post-free trade times, the way Americans live in their cities will steadily become the way we Canadians live in our cities. We'll "get" some of what's theirs about cities, and we'll lose some of what's ours. This is one impressive reason to be very concerned about the free trade agreement.

"American Cities"! I first think of blighted urban cores: the abandoned, scary, burned-out zones of Detroit, or the dusty and dark corners of once thriving northeastern urban city ports. These are the "deindustrialized" American cities that have seen their skilled workers laid off from factories – victims of the shifting production patterns of multinational corporations as they jump trade and tax barriers like so many Olympics hurdlers.

Another image is the high-rise jungle. Wasn't that phrase invented in New York? Canadian planners and politicians alike claim that we have avoided the Manhattan city-style. We've also, it is said, stayed consciously away from the legendary spaghetti expressways of sprawling Los Angeles. Public transit, that's the Canadian way. We have three times the public transit of American cities, measured according to revenue miles per capita. The flip side of the transportation coin shows that U.S. cities have four times the expressways that we do in our cities, based on the lane-miles (lane-kilometres!) per person.

On another front, there's a dramatic difference because U.S. city cores have been losing their children while we have been bringing them back. Canadian cities want to keep their families living downtown. Our cities are better places for children as a result.

As John Sewell reminds us, we also live closer together in Canadian cities – they are more dense. Maybe it's just that "up north" we have to keep warm. Actually, because of our public transit emphasis, Canadians want to live closer to the bus or subway service, which is concentrated

139

■■■■■■■■■■■■■■■■■■■■■■■■■■■■■■■■

and focused. In the States, the sprawling suburb flows directly from the ubiquity of the car. Part of the explanation is a subtle difference in values. Public transit is collective travel. A streetcar or bus is almost a moving community. At least it is compared to a car. The car is an ultimate form of individualism: it's you against the rest. Your car is your identity, your armour in the rush-hour battle. Nothing is more American.

These are also issues of urban form and structure. If there's one unifying theme in all Canadian urban planning rhetoric it has been that we want to ''avoid the problems of the American cities.'' We haven't really avoided these pitfalls totally. But we've been sufficiently successful that Canadian cities are said to be cities that ''work.''

Free trade will inexorably force the urban structure of U.S. cities into our own because the marriage of economic systems brings the union of economic processes: deindustrialization, urban development patterns, transportation systems. In the States, General Motors bought and then closed down public transit systems a few decades ago. It hasn't had the chance in Canada – yet. Will anyone be surprised when Congress claims that monthly transit passes are hidden and unfair subsidies to Canadian workers?

With free trade, as well, our cities will ''get'' inequality. The extremes of wealth and poverty in U.S. cities are legendary. In fact, I think we've already started down a similar road in the biggest Canadian cities. When I make my way home in downtown Toronto these days, I see more stretch limousines and luxury sports cars than I've ever seen before. At the same time, on the same street, I see more street people trying to squeeze survival out of a life of hostels, stairwells, and food banks. These sights have been commonplace in American cities for years. Worse, they've become accepted images there – inevitable and permanent.

In Canadian cities, at least, people are saying that we must fight homelessness and poverty: we say homes and

140

▪▪▪▪▪▪▪▪▪▪▪▪▪▪▪▪▪▪▪▪▪▪▪▪▪▪▪▪▪▪▪

jobs should replace hostels and food banks. So it's not only the inequality itself, it's the acceptance of inequality that I fear most. America too often blames its victims. Canadians are noticeably less likely to wash their hands.

The part of the vision of American cities most in focus for me is violence. I just don't feel nearly as safe walking along a big city street in the States as I do strolling on a Canadian city sidewalk. I'm not alone. American visitors tell us the same thing. During Caribana Festival in Toronto, black Detroit visitors always start their standard Toronto rave with the safe (and clean) streets. No wonder. Detroit has twenty times as many murders each year as Toronto! Statistics have consistently found violent crime levels per thousand population to be five times higher in the U.S. than in Canada.

"Wait! How could free trade breed increased urban violence?" pipes up the sceptic. Urban violence in all its forms is a symptom of deeper problems, of pressures, conflicts, and severe tensions in the way the cities and city folk work and live. Crime flows from the contradictions between rich and poor, from the deep frustrations of the unemployed, and from the insecurities of those pushed from or kept out of the mainstream without an adequate social services security net to soften the hard edges of their lives and to provide at least minimal security and protection from deprivation. In Canada, the extremes are not as great. The difference is noticeable and important.

Another source of the violence is cultural: violence in the U.S. is institutionalized through a widespread military legitimacy. It is all too often celebrated and wrapped in good-versus-evil imagery through constant media assaults. Will Canadian city kids experience more or less of this troublesome, simplistic world view after the trade accord?

We'll also get racism. Even as a white, I can feel it in almost every city south of the border to which I've travelled. The economic segregation in housing neighbour-

■■■■■■■■■■■■■■■■■■■■■■■■■■■■■■■■■

hoods or ghettoes is startling. You don't feel that you're in a multiracial city, as you do in Toronto. It's a feeling, instead, of separation of races. I know that this is felt strongly by my friends of colour. Free trade producing urban racism? This sounds a bit far-fetched perhaps, but basic attitudes and values, especially ones as deep-seated as racism, are reflections of our socio-economic systems. Classic unbridled capitalism, so celebrated south of the border, is in good measure responsible for the lower level of tolerance.

Much of the gulf that lies between the two countries' cities flows out of the strictly competitive economic structures that almost exclusively dominate the life of America's cities. In Canada there is a political culture and even an economic ethos that retain a certain collective sense of responsibility. You can find it many places: from the concept of the crown corporation or the city-run housing program to medical and unemployment insurance. We still need more of this way of thinking in our city politics, but we're sure to be permitted less under free trade.

The "Americanization" of Canada and its cities is not a new process. Several of the trends discussed here are already more or less upon us. In my mind there is absolutely no question that the dramatic and explicit integration embodied in free trade will accelerate their arrival. If allowed to proceed, our already challenging job to make our cities healthy and livable for all will certainly become much more difficult under the continental urban economic order. Let's not make it harder on ourselves.

CANADA LABELLED A "TRUST TERRITORY" OF U.S.

■ ■

". . . the East-West flow has always made sense to Canada."

William Loewen

William Loewen is the founder and chairman of Comcheq Services Limited, a national payroll service company with its head office in Winnipeg. For the past decade he has been involved in transborder data-processing.

Part of the dissatisfaction of Canadians with the status quo lies in the idea that Canadians would be better off if the main economic flows in North America were North-South rather than East-West. My argument makes the case that the East-West flow has always made sense to Canada, that it is much better than the alternative, and that we must retain our ability to maintain it and expand it to meet the needs of existing and emerging technologies.

In the early days, the rivers and lakes were the communication systems that supported the commerce of our country. That single fact dictated to a large degree the

■■■■■■■■■■■■■■■■■■■■■■■■■■■

political divisions that evolved. Once these dividends had been established, technological advancements were forced to follow the same pattern. Railways, the trans-Canada telephone system, and the Trans-Canada highway all came into being to replace the use of U.S. facilities that had been filling those needs. The East-West flow also made Winnipeg the gateway to the West. And, without it, the American cities along the Canadian border would have developed more rapidly and become more important, and our prairie cities would have been considerably smaller. The Ontario industrial-based heartland would have little if any access to the western Canadian market. The evolution of the grain movement system would have seen western produce reaching the ocean via the Mississippi rather than the St. Lawrence Seaway, which probably would not have been built. There would be no Crow's Nest Pass rates to ensure use of the rail system as it did exist. The Panama Canal would carry more eastern Canadian products to the West and vice versa. Vancouver would likely receive more imports for the western economy but ship fewer of its exports. The total western Canadian economy would be much smaller than it is today due largely to being serviced by non-Canadian facilities.

The point I am trying to make here is that this portion of the continent has become a much more highly developed economy than it would have, had a laissez-faire approach been taken by Canadians. There is no need for my present purpose to carry this speculation into the political possibilities that might also have ensued.

The shape and size of the United States makes for a compact, well-rounded economic unit. To rely on natural economic forces coming principally from the U.S. to develop the Canadian portion of this continent never made sense and never will. Their interests could never be anything but exploitative, just as they are now. If western Canadians feel hard done by the East now, we would be much worse off if we were dependent on decisions

emanating from the focal point of a North-South economy. Once again, we Canadians have done a much better
job of developing this portion of the continent without the
U.S. than would have been the case had we settled for
the North-South economy that some advocate.

Over the past few years we have attempted to redress
this East-West flow in favour of a North-South one. Trade
with the U.S. has expanded quite significantly, but in spite
of this, unemployment has remained very high in Canada.
This is because, as was predicted by Sir John A. Macdonald, the job content of our natural resource exports is
low. A straight-line projection of the current economic
situation is such that, the more we trade with United
States, the more difficult become our employment problems. Eventually, of course, this must reflect in a smaller
population.

It would be unfortunate if Canada were to fail to maintain its East-West economy at this particular time. We are
in the midst of revolution of some scope in our industrial
and commercial procedures. This revolution has been
brought on by the computer and its integration into communication systems. Such a change is an opportunity to
create new industries and new wealth within this country.

While many of our existing and older industries have
become foreign-owned, these new businesses offer an
opportunity to change the balance in favour of Canadian
ownership. Unrestricted access of U.S. firms to our market, both in terms of sale of their manufactured goods
and, much more importantly, in terms of their sale of
services via communication systems, will deny Canadians many of the opportunities that should be retained for
them.

The trade agreement provides that access in the most
comprehensive terms imaginable. It ensures that the
Canadian services market will be dominated by U.S.
firms, which inevitably have more opportunities to be the
first entrants into many of these new markets. It ensures
that the existing and future East-West facilities necessary

■ ■

for Canadians to serve themselves will not be built or will be used at a high cost because of limited volume.

Four distinct economies will emerge from this break-down of our East-West communications systems: the western provinces, Ontario, Quebec, and the Maritimes and Newfoundland. The language barrier provides a shield that may allow Quebec industries to thrive in spite of removal of other barriers. This will be particularly helpful to emerging industries. The other areas of Canada can expect isolation from one another and a lower rate of economic activity. Having no particular *raison d'être* in a North-South economy, these economic regions can only survive with lower population, lower standard of living, or both – just as they would have experienced had there never been an East-West economy.

"Under the label of 'free trade' Canada is being asked to support an unprecedented surrender of our resources."

Ian McDougall

Ian McDougall teaches at Osgoode Hall Law School in Toronto. He specializes in commercial, oil and gas, and aerospace law. He is the author of numerous articles on trade and resource-related issues.

It is possible to support multilateral free trade and be firmly opposed to the current agreement. First of all, the purported "free trade deal" is an exercise in misleading advertising. On the trade side it accomplishes no more than a number of highly specific changes to the existing trading relationship. It is piecemeal, not comprehensive. As such, it will disappoint both advocates and opponents of free trade alike. But its substantial impact is none-theless breathtaking in at least one sphere. Under the guise of a trade agreement we are being given a full-blown Continental Energy Package. If the government's description of the "elements" of the agreement is accu-

■■■■■■■■■■■■■■■■■■■■■■■■■■■■■■■■

rate, to call this "free trade" is like putting a "War and Peace" jacket around a Harold Robbins novel and then doubling the sticker price for good measure. The government seems to be betting that the country doesn't read.

What the government is proposing is that we give the United States unrestricted access to Canadian reserves of oil and gas and other sources of energy without regard to the international border. On our behalf the government is prepared to promise the Americans that Canada will eliminate reserves held back for security of supply purposes and that we will never attempt to regulate domestic prices such that Canadians pay less for their own supplies than do Americans.

The magnitude of this concession is staggering to the point of humiliation. Our allegedly hard-fought agreement is an achievement for which the American negotiators can be justly proud. Given what has been accomplished, any suggestions from the Mulroney government that this will be a "hard sell" in the U.S. are about as credible as would have been a refusal by the U.S. to ratify the Louisiana Purchase. On what possible basis would the U.S. refuse a resource concession given in the name of relatively trivial readjustments to the Canada-U.S. trading relationship, which of themselves may end up positive from the American vantage point?

To appreciate the energy package some historical context is useful. In the early part of the century Canada learned bitter lessons as a result of excessive gas and hydroelectric power commitments to U.S. export markets. The shortages that resulted precipitated an effective ban on power and fuel exports for close to fifty years. At the time it was felt that Canada had to treat such matters with extreme caution: our climate makes adequacy of supplies as critical to survival as it is to future industrial growth.

When the first oil and gas discoveries were made in western Canada in the forties and fifties we began to re-evaluate the position of exports. Geographic barriers between domestic markets and the Alberta and British Columbia discoveries were formidable, and the possibility of U.S. exports was attractive if they could provide the basis for initial development, add to the commercial diversification of the western economic base, and hasten the construction of pipelines connecting western production to the large industrial markets of Vancouver, southwest Ontario, and Quebec. In short, exports that helped Canadians gain access to western oil and gas were to be encouraged so long as trends of discovery continued to ensure that future supplies were not in doubt.

The early export sales became the subject of political controversy because of concerns as to the fairness of the prices being paid by U.S. customers, the complete absence of regulatory controls, and the financing of the various pipeline projects involved, particularly the Trans-Canada gas pipeline from Alberta to Toronto.

This debate was a large factor in the electoral success of John Diefenbaker in 1957. He was determined to control the many problems connected with the export sales, and, through the Borden Royal Commission, created the National Energy Board to oversee and regulate exports. Hereafter, exports were subject to a "surplus test" to ensure adequate supplies for Canadian consumers. Pricing was also controlled to ensure that revenues bore some sensible relationship to prices being paid by Canadians.

While the National Energy Board's history has been plagued with debate about its effectiveness, the importance of its presence has never been in doubt. During the OPEC embargo and the subsequent increases in the world price of oil, the role of the NEB, both as an adviser to the federal government and as a regulator of the industry, expanded dramatically.

Canada again had to absorb painful lessons through the "energy crisis." It became suddenly clear that our base of commercially available supplies of both gas and oil was limited and that our frontier wealth remained commercially hypothetical. Future production from either the tarsands or the Canada Lands was going to be very high-cost and take a decade or more to tap. We also learned that our position as an oil importer was precarious and that a large interruption in international supplies could seriously expose large Canadian markets. As a result, three priorities emerged. First, Canada extended the market reach of western energy to help offset the reliance on potentially unstable international supplies. Second, to fend off a recession, the government cushioned consumers and industries from the full and immediate impact of the OPEC-driven price increases through an administered pricing system. And third, a scheme of incentives was implemented to encourage exploration of Canada Lands in the hope that new sources would be discovered and developed to offset the alarming depletion of the western Canadian reserves.

This was, of course, the much debated National Energy Program. It was a fractious era from the standpoint of federal-provincial relations. It was also crisis-driven. All concerned, the private oil and gas sector included, believed that oil and gas prices would continue to escalate toward fifty dollars a barrel and beyond. All believed that massive fiscal intervention was necessary in the form of tax relief and other incentives. Where the federal government had once restrained prices, there was a growing sense that in future it might be necessary to impose artificially higher prices in order to justify commercially the high costs of exploration and production. In short, the need for government to be involved was never in doubt. The debate instead centred on where effort and expenditure should be concentrated and which level of government should predominate. It was a period of crisis that has every likelihood of being repeated in the not-distant future, and with it would come the need for another series of massive governmental/regulatory interventions.

We have short memories, however, about the speed and severity of the onset of the 1973 energy crisis. It has every prospect of returning, but when it does we will be totally

■■■■■■■■■■■■■■■■■■■■■■■■■■■■■■

unprepared because most of the critical regulatory mechanisms have been dismantled. Beginning in 1983 the bottom began to fall out of the oil market. OPEC ceased being the invincible cartel it had seemed in the mid-1970s. Prices retreated to the point that frontier developments were commercially impossible. The recession-led market shrinkage in turn dramatically reduced industry revenues. And the United States introduced a series of measures that cut into the Canadian share of the market at the very moment when producers were trying to increase export levels and were appealing for price reductions to offset competition from their U.S. counterparts. In a nutshell, the pressure was off from the standpoint of supply security and high prices. But it was a predicament that called for real leadership. While it appeared that we were suddenly swimming in a sea of gas and oil, the reality was every bit as serious as it was in the era of general crisis. The stocks of conventional (or available) supplies were unchanged, but the producers and the producing provinces wanted to double exports to make up for the fall in revenues that had been caused by the fall in prices. This, of course, meant that depletion rates were bound to rise and future requirements inevitably would be compromised.

The then-new Mulroney government took the occasion to initiate a series of sweeping retreats from the National Energy Program. The NEP was rightly branded as inappropriate for the new conditions of low prices and free-flowing international supplies of oil. But the change in circumstances did not include any significant increases to Canada's available base of oil and natural gas, and the need to protect existing supplies and to encourage frontier development still remained, notwithstanding the deterioration in commercial prospects. To yield to the pressure to increase exports was to guarantee a loss of Canada's commercially accessible gas reserves for future domestic use.

Under the guise of "deregulation" we abandoned price

153

controls and the incentives for frontier development, and
began the process of systematically reducing the level of
protection for Canadian consumers in order to increase
the amounts available for export to the United States at
the new lower prices. It was suggested that if large con-
suming provinces like Ontario had a problem with this
they could go out and buy up reserves in the ground rather
than rely on government to do the job for them. In short,
Ontario consumers should compete with consumers from
California for anything above the bare minimal protection
levels sustained by the NEB under the Canadian reserve
requirements formula.

Instead of providing leadership, the government
encouraged the NEB simply to rewrite the rules so that
requirements for future Canadians would be lowered and
the amounts declared currently "surplus" would be artificially increased. In this context, the free trade agreement is the mechanism for altogether abandoning any
level of protection. In one stroke the exporters will have
a vast increase in the quantity of Canadian gas available
for U.S. export. It will be the cause of future regret.

As far as hydroelectric power and nuclear power are
concerned, the agreement will permit the provinces to
make unlimited commitments to the U.S. market. This is
a popular move so far as Quebec and British Columbia
are concerned. In geopolitical terms, the inclusion of the
energy package in the agreement would almost appear
calculated to secure a higher level of popularity for the
government in the West and Quebec, the two keys to their
re-election strategy. Ontario and the Maritimes are big
losers in this situation.

There are still large unknowns, however. The Columbia River Treaty will expire. Ordinarily, our right to
repatriate the electrical potential committed under the
treaty should be clear. However, the "guaranteed
access" of the U.S. under the agreement may have
clouded our position in this respect.

Under the label of "free trade" Canada is being asked

to support an unprecedented surrender of our resources. The federal government has abandoned its responsibility to manage in the national interest a sector that is critical to a northern nation. It has yielded in favour of the short-term aspirations of producing provinces, and in a manner that appears destined to encourage hostility toward the country's industrial heartland, which will be badly disadvantaged as a result. Moreover, the energy package has been tendered as a complete surprise to the public and at least some of the provinces.

Few can dispute the fact that multilateral liberalization of trading rules is a worthwhile and probably overdue objective. The United States will undoubtedly continue to be an important part of our trading future, but the shift of the global commercial centre of gravity eastward has major implications for Canada as a Pacific Rim trader. This shift can open up large new opportunities for energy trade: particularly as the role of LNG (liquefied natural gas) matures within the East Asian energy supply network. What we are being offered today are a series of limited changes to our trade relations with a single country, and these changes cannot compensate for what is a virtually guaranteed foreign domination of a resource base that successive Canadian governments have attempted to protect for over eighty years.

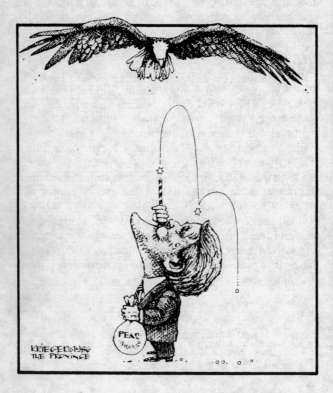

■■■■■■■■■■■■■■■■■■■■■■■■■■■■

"... the provisions on energy

represent a significant loss

for Canada."

Joseph A. Mercier

Born in Saskatchewan, Joseph Mercier ranches southwest of Calgary and is president of Universal Explorations Ltd., an energy company.

My business instincts tell me that I welcome free trade. With better grass, a better climate, fewer bugs, and less disease in these Alberta foothills, I can raise a calf cheaper than my friends further south. Nowhere can I find a better combination of good prospects, stable policies, and efficient information and services than exists in the oil patch of western Canada; so competing in the development of oil and natural gas is no problem. Free trade should allow me a wider selection and lower prices for the machinery, trucks, and automobiles needed in my major occupations. Sometimes I dare to think that it would loosen the control of monopolies in the transportation, refining, and distribution system, thereby

157

encouraging equity and efficiency in the marketing of natural gas and crude oil.

Then why am I so uneasy about the free trade pact? Mostly because the agreement is poorly explained and defended. Our Premier warns us that we had better support it or else. Our federal Energy Minister is amazed that anyone could be against it. To the Deputy Prime Minister it is obvious that any who oppose it do not have the facts. Simon Reisman and the Prime Minister feel hurt that anyone should question its merits; in fact, anyone who does is inward-looking, disloyal, maybe traitorous. Even the usually analytical and perceptive publisher of the *Calgary Herald* wasted a feature article in a tirade of name-calling instead of exploring the issues. Letters to the editor and glossy brochures from Conservative MPs and MLAs have little substance, only the message that the agreement is good and should not be opposed. Why such a "negative sell"? If the Deputy Prime Minister is correct, he can dissipate opposition by simply providing the facts. He doesn't do so, and the suspicion grows that this free trade agreement is seriously flawed.

The actual agreement is overdue, so analysis can only be done on the various drafts of the "Elements of the Agreement." Generally, I get the impression that Canada is required to make more substantial changes than is the U.S. and that it must make its changes sooner. The Americans appear to enjoy more important exceptions. They also seem indifferent to the motherhood promises made in the agreement. In the section on agriculture, each party has "agreed to take into account the export interests of the other party in the use of any export subsidy on agricultural goods exported to third world countries . . . ." A paragraph entitled "Standstill" recognized that both parties must exercise discretion while approval of the agreement is being sought on both sides of the border. American attempts to capture traditional Canadian markets for wheat by offering subsidies to Canada's customers would appear to contravene the agreement even before it is signed.

In my view, the provisions on energy represent a significant loss for Canada. Americans will buy our crude oil and natural gas with or without an agreement. Our exports of natural gas are impeded somewhat by the ever-present "Gas Bubble" or surplus and limited transportation and distribution facilities. A free trade agreement won't change that. But there is a significant change to the country as a whole. In an effort to pave the way for a free trade arrangement, Canada dismantled the National Energy Program and weakened the Foreign Investment Review Agency. In "Elements of the Agreement" it goes much further. It agrees to change its laws and restrict the authority of its bureaucrats. The National Energy Board now has little reason to exist. Independent producers have frequently disagreed with its findings but they have always had a chance to be heard and they have come to know and respect the officials. No more. The National Energy Board can no longer make rulings affecting the energy needs of Canadian producers and consumers.

For these concessions and tokens of good faith and for granting the Americans unlimited access to our energy resources and equities, Canada obtained little for its energy sector. We did not obtain the right to compete in the American market on the same basis as the American producer. While Canada dismantled programs objectionable to its neighbour, its neighbour imposed a tariff on Canadian crude oil and punitive restrictions on natural gas. The Federal Energy and Resources Commission in the U.S. remains intact, as do its rulings. So do all other American regulatory bodies having jurisdiction over transportation, distribution, and marketing of natural gas. For the American side, the preliminary agreement grandfathers the "status quo," possibly including new measures that may be passed prior to January 1, 1989, under the Congress Protection Bill. The "superfund" portion of the tariff on crude oil may go. It was illegal under current agreements and should have gone under appeal in any event. The balance of the tariff remains.

If there are any benefits to Canadians they are few and highly questionable. A prohibition of entry of Alaskan crude into Canada will be lifted to the extent of 50,000 barrels a day. Surely this must have been inserted as a token concession. Who wants to import Alaskan crude? Certainly not western Canadian producers or eastern Canadian refiners. Conceivably, a West Coast refinery might benefit. If it does, under this "free trade" agreement, it had better ensure that American ships transport the crude. If this concession and a possible reduction of tariffs on petrochemicals are all we have obtained, and there are no balancing provisions in other sectors, then we gave up too much in the energy sector.

From an energy point of view, the most concerted argument for free trade is that a free trade agreement will prevent future governments in Ottawa from implementing national energy programs. Many of my associates, beset by current problems in our oil and gas industry, can never forgive Ontario for their losses under the NEP. Few remember that our former Premier clinked champagne glasses with our former Prime Minister in accepting the NEP. Few remember that with the perception of ever higher prices, the provincial and federal governments were similarly indecent in their race to grab proceeds at the expense of the industry. Most would rather take their chances on government interference from Washington or state capitals than risk having eastern Canada pillage them again.

Moreover, southern Alberta is strongly influenced by Americans. Many Albertans are employed by American major companies. Those who aren't are heavily influenced by the majors in industry associations and in business transactions. Few Calgarians, depending on the industry for their living, are likely to antagonize their employers or clients. Corporate expenditures in sponsoring high-profile artistic and athletic events enhance the

■■■■■■■■■■■■■■■■■■■■■■■■■■■■■■

image of the American majors. So do contributions to political parties. As a result, the voice of the oil industry is an American voice, and it strongly supports the free trade agreement.

Free trade is an attractive idea, but this agreement as we know it now doesn't appear to provide a balanced arrangement. Nor did the negotiations. Our people negotiated from a position of weakness. While they and our federal government made one concession after another, protectionist forces in the United States were applying pressure with adverse rulings on our products – hydrocarbons, softwood, steel, and potash. The result is a weak agreement from a Canadian perspective. That the oil patch is willing to accept it is not surprising. For many of its members, keeping Ontario's hands off Alberta resources is the goal and free trade is the means to achieve it. I don't agree. We can resolve our differences without risking our sovereignty by giving up so much control of our future to unknown bureaucrats in Washington.

■ ■

''We may be negotiating a free trade deal with the wrong partner.''

Peter C. Newman

Peter C. Newman was editor-in-chief of The Toronto Star *and editor of* Maclean's *magazine. He is one of Canada's most renowned and prolific authors. He contributes a weekly column on economic matters to* Maclean's *from his home in Cordova Bay, B.C.*

''What crashed was more than just the market. It was the Reagan Illusion: the idea that there could be a defense buildup and tax cuts without a price, that the country could live beyond its means indefinitely. The initial Reagan years, with their aura of tinseled optimism, had restored the nation's tattered pride and lost sense that leadership was possible in the presidency. But he stayed a term too long. As he shouted befuddled Hooverisms over the roar of his helicopter last week or doddered precariously through his press conference, Reagan appeared embarrassingly irrelevant to a reality that he could scarcely comprehend.''

163

That devastating comment on the recent stock market meltdown was published not in a radical journal or some marginal tract. It was the lead story in the November 2, 1987, issue of *Time*, the house organ of the American Dream, whose founder, the late Henry Luce, had originally decreed the American Century.

His successors were now writing its epitaph.

Over the past weeks, Wall Street analysts have tried to put many faces on the stock market debacle, but its root cause is obvious: a global loss of confidence in the economic and political leadership of the United States of America. By entwining our own destiny with that of the bewildered Gulliver to the south of us, we could become a hostage to its present and future misfortunes.

Such dissent to the current free trade agreement flows not so much from my background as one of the founding members of the Committee for an Independent Canada as from my studies of the avalanche-like decline of the American political economy. We may be negotiating a free trade deal with the wrong partner. If by some unhappy chance the deal as it now stands were to go through, Canada would become the unwilling victim of an economic undertow that would drown our chances for orderly growth and long-term prosperity.

While few Canadians seem concerned about this essential aspect of the current negotiations, thoughtful Americans are well aware of the fragility of their economy. H. Ross Perot, the Texas billionaire, compared October's stock market slide to the minor earthquake that took place at about the same time in Los Angeles – claiming that both events drew attention to tremendous stresses along fundamental fault lines. "It's outrageous that our elected officials claim all the fundamentals of our economy are sound," he complained. "*None* of the fundamentals are sound."

An equally devastating but more detailed critique was voiced in a recent essay by Peter G. Peterson in *The Atlantic*. A stalwart of the American Business Establishment,

■■■■■■■■■■■■■■■■■■■■■■■■■■■■■■

Peterson was chief executive officer of Bell & Howell, served as Secretary of Commerce in Washington, and for eleven years headed Lehman Brothers, New York's most influential merchant bank. His analysis of the American economy portrays that once mighty republic as an overgrown Zambia. "We have transformed ourselves from the world's largest creditor into the world's largest debtor," he laments. "Despite four years of extraordinary luck on the energy front, we have managed to twist the global economy into the most lopsided imbalance between saving (foreign) and spending (American) ever witnessed in the industrialized era. . . . Eight years ago, no one imagined an austerity-led shift toward U.S. isolationism. Now we're seeing it: an attempt to stand tall on bended knees."

According to Peterson and others, the real (as opposed to inflation-fed) U.S. standard of living has hardly budged upward for several decades. While the demise of the British Empire took more than three-quarters of a century to become apparent (as annual increases in productivity dropped below those of its industrial competitors), the decline in American productivity is proceeding at least three times as fast. The actual figures are startling. Between 1979 and 1986, the U.S. investment rate has been the second lowest in the industrialized world and the rate of growth in net output per worker has averaged about 0.4 per cent a year – the lowest of any industrialized state and, incidentally, less than one-fifteenth of what the Japanese were experiencing thirty years ago. Such is the domestic legacy of Reaganomics – a form of fiscal hocuspocus that is less pre-Keynesian than pre-Cambrian.

And that's only on the domestic front. The overall U.S. trade deficit at the end of 1986 was $264 billion, and unless drastic counter-measures are taken, it will reach $400 billion by year's end. That dramatic turnaround, representing half a trillion dollars' worth of borrowing from abroad, dwarfs even the bank recycling that followed the OPEC-inspired surpluses of the early and mid-

■■■■■■■■■■■■■■■■■■■■■■■■■■■■■■■■

1970s. The loss of American economic supremacy looks even worse when examined by sectors. The U.S. now has a significant deficit in high-technology trade, and the balance in manufactured goods has shifted from a $176 billion surplus in 1980 to a $139 billion deficit in 1986.

These signs of economic incompetence and psychic overindulgence are bad enough. But the future looks even worse.

The cumulative U.S. national debt amounted to $645 billion from the time the *Mayflower*'s starboard lookout first sighted the Plymouth shores to the day Ronald Reagan became president. By the time his term expires, that burdensome debt load will have tripled. Any nation faced with such astronomical fiscal liabilities must take drastic remedies. If, by the time those draconian but essential cures are put into effect, our economy has been folded into that of the U.S. – we could be fatally affected.

The motivating hunger on the American side of the proposed free trade deal mostly has to do with gaining unimpeded access to Canadian energy sources. Because the pace of domestic American oil production and discovery has been dropping precipitously, its dependence on petroleum imports has been predicted to increase from the current 25 per cent to 60 per cent during the next decade. Only by tapping into our oil pools can the Americans be assured of continuity of continental supplies.

So there it is – by pinning our economic star to the U.S. we may be hooking on to a plummeting meteor.

Historically, Canada has been a fusion, or rather a living-together, of French Canadians and those United Empire Loyalists who left the Thirteen Colonies after the Revolutionary War because they opted for England and King George. They were joined by waves of Scottish, Irish, and European immigrants seeking to replace oppressions with opportunities. Born out of many defeats, Canada achieved a form of independence in 1867, though its foreign policies were still dictated by Whitehall. Full freedom in international dealings came

■■■■■■■■■■■■■■■■■■■■■■■■■■■■■■■■

only in 1931, and it wasn't until 1949 that the judicial committee of the Privy Council in London ceased to be the final appeal from Canadian courts. This prolonged dependence persuaded an impatient generation of Canadians that the umbilical cord with England could be cut only if Canada were aligned with the United States through closer military, economic, and social ties. And so we went directly from being surrogate Englishmen to being surrogate Americans.

Still cocooned in that colonial status of feeling once removed, we are in real danger of forgetting who we are and why we are here. "Canada," W.L. Morton noted a long time ago, "is not a second-rate United States, still less a United States that failed. Canadian history is rather an important chapter in a distinct and even unique human endeavour: the civilization of a northern and arctic land. Because of its separate origin on the northern frontier, Canadian life is marked by a northern quality and a strong seasonal rhythm. The line which marks off the frontier from the farmstead, the wilderness from the baseland, the hinterland from the metropolis, runs through every Canadian psyche."

That's a quality well worth preserving. The real trouble with free trade is that we may not realize what we've lost until it's too late to get it back.

The process is all too reminiscent of that wonderful old James Thurber cartoon in which a decapitated swordsman, protesting that he is fit to carry on the duel, is told to try sneezing.

"U.S. military planners view Canada the way boxers view their gloves."

David Lorge Parnas

David Parnas is professor of computer science at Queen's University in Kingston, Ontario. After spending many years as an active consultant for the U.S. Defence Department, particularly in battle management, he came to Canada.

The major powers are engaged in a frantic race to develop new arms. Canada's participation in this activity has been relatively restrained, but there are signs that it may grow. The free trade agreement increases the danger for Canada.

It is important to recognize that the Canadian government is attempting to solve a real and serious problem for Canada. The trade problem is real. Canada's economy is heavily dependent on trade with the United States. Much of Canada's productive capacity is devoted to producing goods that will be consumed in the U.S. but not in this country. Many goods essential or important to Canadians are not produced in this country but in the United States. Were the U.S. to introduce new legislation or regulations that interfered with trade between the two countries, serious disruptions would be experienced in Canada. Because the U.S. economy is so much larger, the effects of reduced trade on the U.S. would be much less significant. Consequently, the U.S. is in a position to exert pressure on Canada, asking it to co-operate in military and political activities. When the U.S. asks Canada to make changes, such as the stumpage system in the lumber industry, it is very difficult for Canada to say no. Through trade, Canada has already lost some of its sovereignty.

This problem has not been created by the present government. Many previous governments allowed it to develop. The present government is to be praised for recognizing, and attempting to solve, this problem. The government sought an agreement that would guarantee Canadian access to the U.S. market, providing protection against ''the flood of protectionist legislation'' being introduced to the U.S. Congress. Were an ironclad agreement of this nature in force, the U.S. could not use economic pressure to blackmail Canada.

Unfortunately, the agreement that has been announced does not provide protection against economic blackmail by new legislation. The ''binding disputes settlement mechanism'' can only interpret legislation. It cannot protect against new legislation. The agreement does not define key terms and there are no binding restrictions on the ability of the U.S. Congress to introduce legislation. My experience within the U.S. governmental system leads me to doubt that the U.S. legislators would ever accept limitations on their right to make trade legislation. Further, either side can pull out of the agreement on relatively short notice. Trade with the U.S. is so important to Canada that Canada would be reluctant to pull out, but the relationship is not symmetric. In trade between two countries whose economies differ considerably in magnitude, the larger country is more able to withstand the

■■■■■■■■■■■■■■■■■■■■■■■■■■■■

cancellation of an agreement than the smaller country. The U.S. ability to use trade as a pressure on Canada would not be diminished by the proposed agreement.

Not only does the proposed agreement not provide the necessary protection, it will make the problem worse. Canadian dependence on U.S. markets and U.S. supplies will increase. Whenever Canadian companies win trade battles and sell more to the U.S., Canada becomes more dependent on exports and more subject to pressure such as that exerted in the softwood situation. Whenever Canadian companies lose the trade battles, Canada becomes more dependent on U.S. supplies. Whatever happens in the trade battles, U.S. ability to exert pressure on Canada increases.

U.S. military planners see great strategic value in Canadian territory, energy, and other natural resources. For example, within the U.S. Strategic Defense Initiative, better known as "Star Wars," most plans recognize the value of "forward basing." This concept calls for the basing of a variety of military installations "as far north as possible." Northern territory would be patrolled by Airborne Optical Sensors. Critical ground communications stations on northern territory would connect orbiting battle stations. According to publicly available documents, however, the nuclear "X-Ray Laser" would not be based in space but would "pop-up" from northern waters and northern ground stations when needed. Sensors and computer systems needed for interception of missiles would be based in the North as well. These installations would be primary targets if the U.S.S.R. were ever to attempt to overcome North American defences. Every SDI installation in Canada would be the centre of a "bull's eye" on Soviet maps.

Even when no equipment is based in Canada, U.S. military equipment can pose a threat to Canada. Canadians should never forget that the now "mothballed" Safeguard missile defence system was designed to intercept Soviet missiles over Canadian territory. Because Safe-

171

guard missiles were "nuclear tipped," a nuclear explosion over Canada would have been used to prevent nuclear explosions over the U.S. U.S. military planners view Canada the way boxers view their gloves. You do not protect your gloves; they take a beating to protect you.

U.S. military and political planners take it for granted that Canada's territory is available for their use. One high-ranking planner explained forward basing to me by saying, "If you look at the world from above the North Pole, you see the U.S.S.R. on one side and the U.S. on the other." As the U.S. wastes more and more of its own resources on unusable weapons, it will need more from Canada. To use a phrase from old U.S. recruiting posters: Canada, "Uncle Sam Wants YOU!"

Many Canadians are unaware of how the military industry pervades and controls the U.S. If you stand at a counter in a major U.S. airport and talk to others who are waiting, you will find that a very large number of them are working directly, or indirectly, for the military on arms developments. Even non-military manufacturers sell a large proportion of their production to military suppliers. It is sad but true that the U.S. cannot afford peace. Anyone who is around Washington for a while realizes that the military industry is the most powerful single force in U.S. society. Americans have become captives of the "military industrial complex" that former President Eisenhower warned them about. It is the most heavily subsidized, and inefficient, industry imaginable. Leading economists feel that it is draining the U.S. economy and many concerned citizens fear that it is turning the world into a tinder box.

Canada already engages in arms trade with the U.S., but there are barriers to slow that trade down. First, the arms industry has successfully lobbied against heavy dependence on foreign suppliers, and many rules encourage use of an American source of supply. Whenever someone in the U.S. Defence Department wants to buy something from Canada, a significant amount of extra

172

■■■■■■■■■■■■■■■■■■■■■■■■■■■■■

paperwork must be prepared to justify use of foreign supply. This discourages some contracting officers. The reduction of trade barriers between the two countries will reduce, perhaps even eliminate, the barriers to greater Canadian participation in the U.S. arms industry. Arms themselves appear to be an exception to some of the rules, but the components and materials will not be. It is to be expected that Canada's dependence on the arms industry will increase as a result of both the trade agreement and the policies outlined in the White Paper on Defence. Canada could eventually become another captive of the arms industry. Leading U.S. economists believe that the diversion of resources to the arms industry has seriously damaged the U.S. economy. The trade agreement could lead Canada into the same trap.

We all know the song from *Oklahoma*, "I'm just a girl who can't say no." Canada has often been in that position in the past few years. Canada has been reduced to dealing with American regulatory bodies at the same level as American corporations. With the proposed elimination of restrictions in foreign investment, and elimination of duties, this situation will become worse. That amusing song from *Oklahoma* could become Canada's *de facto* national anthem.

Canada and the U.S. have agreed to further talks intended to introduce common trade laws and definitions. If, indeed, the U.S. laws are modified to recognize that Canadian social institutions such as UIC are not subsidies, it will be a step forward. However, those talks have not yet started and agreement is far away. In my view, agreement to definitions and rules that favour Canada is very unlikely. On the other hand, the Canadian concessions are quite concrete and begin to take effect when the agreement is effective, not at some vague point in the future.

While I personally believe that Canada would be foolish to allow its territory to be used as the U.S. Department of Defence wants to use it, I recognize that there are Canadians who feel that this is the least of several evils.

173

However, I hope that even those Canadians would want to see Canada able to decide whether or not to be used in this way. Canada must retain enough economic sovereignty to be able to make such decisions without fear of economic devastation. The ability to say "No" is essential to self-respect and self-protection.

The government is correct to try to solve our economic problems. It is within Canada's capability to solve the problems. The solution lies in a restructuring of the Canadian economy so that it is less dependent on U.S. trade. Canada can, and should, produce enough of its "needs" for its own consumption. There is good advice often given to lonely people, "You cannot be good to live with until you can live by yourself." We can gain much by trade with our neighbours, but we lose when we become so desperately dependent on them that they can blackmail us.

Proponents of the proposed agreement accuse the opponents of being cowards, of being afraid that Canada cannot compete. That is not the case; it is obvious to everyone that Canadians can compete. Canadian products sell in other countries even when there are tariff barriers to overcome. It is the opponents of free trade who are positive about Canada. They believe that Canada has the resources, the people, and the initiative to succeed as a self-standing economy and an independent country. It is the supporters of the proposed agreement who are fearful. They believe that Canada could not thrive without more dependence on the U.S.

The debate on this agreement could be a turning point for Canada. Canada can turn toward the U.S., become more dependent on it, become more militarized. Canada could also strengthen its economy and move toward a world in which it determines its own policies. Canada can turn away from dependence on the arms trade. Canada can refuse to be turned into a target in the next major war. Canada can choose the freedom to work for peace.

Adriane Raeside

175

■■■■■■■■■■■■■■■■■■■■■■■■■■■■■

"We don't mind an open economy, we just don't want an empty one."

The Honourable Tony Penikett

Tony Penikett has been leader of Yukon's New Democratic Party government since May, 1985. He is also the minister responsible for the Department of Finance, the Department of Economic Development, and the Public Service Commission. Prior to entering politics, he worked at the Clinton Creek asbestos mine.

The Yukon is a small community in the top left-hand corner of Canada, occupying an area the size of Sweden. One quarter of us are aboriginal and the rest of us are settlers. Sixty per cent of us live in Whitehorse, our capital city, and the rest in a dozen communities spread across the territory.

The Yukon economy is very narrowly based. Three main sectors – mining, government, and services – provide almost all the jobs in the territory. We have very small manufacturing and underdeveloped forestry, fishery, and farming sectors.

■■■■■■■■■■■■■■■■■■■■■■■■■■■■■■■

In the recession that ravaged the Yukon between 1982 and 1985, there was a point at which all of our mines were closed, our population had dropped by 10 per cent, employment had dropped by 15 per cent, unemployment rates had almost doubled, construction had almost been cut in half, and retail sales were down considerably. Almost every economic indicator showed we were in real trouble.

Elected in May, 1985, our government responded to the immediate crisis by making job creation our top priority. Within six months we had negotiated a development agreement with private investors and the federal government to reopen our biggest mine, at Faro. This lead-zinc property by itself had once represented 40 per cent of our gross territorial product, and its return to production created a thousand jobs.

We also directed tens of millions of dollars into new public works: roads, schools, and community services. This put hundreds more back to work. The Yukon's economic history is a series of booms: the Klondike gold rush, the Alaska Highway construction, mining booms and the busts that followed. Transients have always profited in the good times, while the locals suffered in the bad. So we developed strong local-hire, northern-preference, and value-added incentive programs to keep some of the benefits of this public spending in our communities.

We continued this approach for the local service sector, with local procurement policies. The territorial government is, after all, the largest customer for many of our small businesses. One interesting experiment in this area involved local furniture manufacturing. Our government discovered that we could purchase high-quality, competitively priced office furniture from local woodwork shops, which were normally inactive during the winter months. This has proved to be a very successful project.

With a recovery under way, we began to address some of our structural weaknesses. Yukon has the leakiest of economies. If you put a dollar into the Yukon economy,

177

a quarter instantly flows south for imported oil, ten cents follows for imported food, and another dime for imported building materials. This obviously represents a massive hemorrhage of jobs, taxes, profits, and potential. We don't mind an open economy, we just don't want an empty one.

To diversify our economy and reduce our dependence on outside goods and services, our government made import substitution a central feature of our economic revival. Local lumber, furniture manufacturing, commercial greenhouse operations, game ranching, and fish farming are some of the ventures we have supported and encouraged to increase the use of import replacements – both to apply the knowledge and skills of local people and to improve the local value added to our economy.

In the energy field we are helping to retrofit private homes and businesses as well as public buildings. We are building a new $50 million college that will be heated with local wood, coal, and garbage. As an alternative to oil, we are promoting hydro projects in rural areas and waste-wood central heating plants in our towns. As well, to better control our electrical rates and improve services to Yukon consumers, our government bought the Yukon assets of the Northern Canada Power Commission from the federal government. Control of this major utility will provide Yukoners with a powerful economic tool that is sensitive to local needs and requirements.

The government is the largest builder in the territory, so we decided that in future we would use local materials in our structures. Rather than importing steel and glass and specialized labour to put up imitation Vancouver skyscrapers, we would take advantage of our wide-open spaces and as much as possible build low-profile buildings with Yukon forest products. This decision is creating jobs for loggers, sawyers, and carpenters in many of our communities. Over time it may, as well, give our architecture a distinctly regional character. We should end

■■■■■■■■■■■■■■■■■■■■■■■■■■■■■■■■

up with buildings that look like they belong on our landscape.

The Yukon has had a colonial economy. The big decisions affecting our lives have always been made someplace else. Our government decided we wanted to change that by developing our own economic strategy. We began a process we call Yukon 2000, a long-range planning exercise to help us chart a course toward the next century. We commissioned dozens of research papers, sectoral studies, and economic environment reports. Through a series of public conferences, community meetings, and sectoral workshops, we met with business people, workers, women, aboriginal people, public employees, educators, developers, volunteers, mayors, and chiefs. We quickly discovered a strong desire by Yukoners to direct and manage our own future. The issue was no longer whether planning was a good or bad thing, the issue was "Who does it?" Yukoners had come to the conclusion that if we didn't plan for ourselves in our own interests, then the federal government, multinational corporations, or someone else would do it for us. We could be sure that if that happened they would be doing it according to their priorities, not according to ours.

So local control emerged as a central theme from our consultations. We decided we should build on our strengths – our flexibility and adaptability – to diversify, to strive for sustainable growth. The result of all these efforts over the last two years is a vibrant, expanding economy: employment has grown by 20 per cent; mining, tourism, and construction are achieving new highs; forestry, furniture, fishing, and farming industries are coming into their own; and our territory is optimistic and confident.

The continental trade deal would take us in another direction. From what we know about the arrangement so far, it might return us to the narrow, weak, and colonial past that our community has rejected. The deal may have serious repercussions for local control and import substitution. In a post-free trade environment, for example, we simply could not have made the deal that reopened the Faro mine. The United States would have screamed "subsidy."

Instead of greater certainty and stability the trade agreement offers us less. Our local-hire and value-added policies would be at risk, and now attempts are already being made to have us sign interprovincial accords to dismantle such policies. Our import substitution initiatives could be in trouble as well. The Canada-U.S. agreement would seriously undermine our efforts to reduce our economy's dependence on and vulnerability to outside economic forces. Cheap food imports could bury our emerging agricultural industry. Our locally manufactured furniture could be replaced by mass-produced alternatives from right-to-work states in America. Northern energy resources are to be treated as southern assets to be traded away to the benefit of the provinces. And, if we can't regulate foreign investment, how do we require developers to buy Yukon supplies, hire aboriginals, or train women? Will the boomers then be back like the swallows of spring to take our jobs?

As Yukoners have tried to diversify our economy within, so we have sought to diversify our economic relations without. Most of our mineral exports are bound for northern Europe and Pacific Rim countries. It is doubtful that a "fortress North America" trading agreement with the United States will do much to strengthen our existing markets.

What we are doing in our region goes very much against the grain of the continental approach to development promoted by free-traders. For years I've joked that when a new mine opened in Yukon, the ore went to Tokyo, the profits went to Toronto or New York, the taxes went to Ottawa, and the jobs went to Vancouver and Edmonton. What we got was a hole in the ground, which, if the federal government gave us permission, we could use as a municipal dump. If that's free trade, we don't want it!

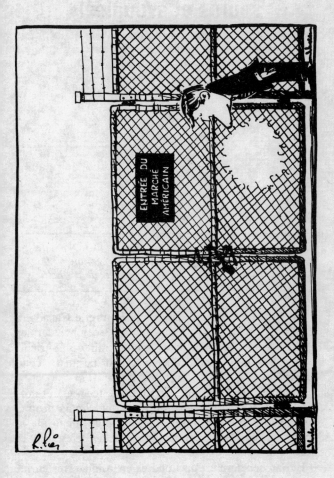

«Nous sommes donc à la fois sourds et aveugles!»

Jacques Proulx

Jacques Proulx est le Président-Général de l'Union des Producteurs Agricoles du Québec, qui regroupe 47,000 producteurs. Il possède une ferme laitière dans l'Estrie.

L'Accord sur le libre-échange signé entre le Canada et les Etats-Unis à minuit moins une le 3 octobre dernier répond d'emblée à notre plus grande crainte : l'agriculture a servi de monnaie d'échange pour permettre cette entente.

Aujourd'hui, les hommes politiques, fédéraux et provinciaux, osent prétendre qu'ils n'ont jamais promis l'exclusion de l'agriculture d'un tel traité, ni même le statut spécial. Nous sommes donc à la fois sourds et aveugles!

En janvier dernier, de Londres en Angleterre, en février de Davos en Suisse, monsieur Bourassa excluait l'agriculture, ce que monsieur Pagé venait de dire égale-

ment. Au congrès de l'UPA, en décembre 1986, monsieur
Roch LaSalle, au nom du gouvernement fédéral, faisait
de même. Monsieur de Cotret, le 30 janvier 87, devant
600 personnes à Trois-Rivières, y allait d'une promesse
identique.

Si aujourd'hui nous faisons référence à ces engage-
ments, c'est que le monde agricole y avait cru. Paraît-il
que cela ne s'appelle pas «mentir». D'accord, mais comment faut-il donc le nommer? Car, ne l'oublions par, pour
les secteurs vraiment exclus de l'Accord, *c'est marqué
noir sur blanc* (industries culturelles, bière, etc.). Notre
analyse précise des textes existants, sous réserve des documents finaux que l'on nous promet dans les trois
semaines, n'a rien de réjouissant. Quand même vou-
drions-nous y chercher une seule mesure bénéfique . . .
il n'y en a pas.

L'élimination de tous les tarifs douaniers agricoles sur
une période maximale de dix ans (page 14 de l'Accord)
ne peut que frapper notre secteur.

Les secteurs de la volaille et des oeufs devront faire
face, immédiatement à l'entrée en vigueur du traité, à une
hausse des quotas d'importation d'une part. Mais, plus
grave, l'abolition des tarifs *supprime 17 %* des frais de
douane à l'importation des produits transformés à haute
valeur ajoutée (page 14 de l'Accord) comme les TV dinners, les pâtés de dinde, etc.

Le tribunal d'arbitrage n'est nullement exécutoire et
ressemble étrangement à une simple cour d'appel qui, par
contre, jugera en regard des lois du pays qui lèvera les
nouvelles taxes compensatoires. Le droit de lever des
taxes compensatoires futures est reconnu et les taxes déjà
en place ne sont pas retirées, donc pas d'accès garanti
au marché américain pour les produits canadiens. Plus
de 90 % des taxes compensatoires sont le fait des
Américains.

Par ailleurs, l'Accord, pour le moins, nous porte à
poser un certain nombre de questions. L'élimination des
tarifs jouera-t-elle sur la gestion des approvisionnements

■■■■■■■■■■■■■■■■■■■■■■■■■■■■■■■

des produits non contingentés, tels le yogourt et la crème glacée? Dans le lait encore, l'on propose «l'abolition de toutes les restrictions quantitatives existantes» (page 5 de l'Accord). Les agences de commercialisation (notamment dans les oeufs d'incubation et la pomme de terre) seront-elles possibles puisque dans les «restrictions générales» (page 4 de l'Accord), il est spécifié que «les deux parties sont convenues qu'elles ne maintiendront ni n'introduiront de restrictions à l'importation»? Tout cela est prévu par le GATT nous dit-on mais, par ailleurs, le Canada, dans l'Accord, accepte d'aligner sa position sur les Américains qui proposent l'abolition totale de toute restriction au commerce. Le Canada pourrait donc allonger sa liste de contingentements, mais alors il contreviendrait à l'esprit de l'Accord qu'il vient de signer avec son voisin.

Le développement, la consolidation et la stabilisation dans le secteur agricole pourront-ils se poursuivre en regard de l'Accord qui stipule «les parties sont convenues que leur premier objectif en regard de l'agriculture est d'éliminer sur une base globale tous les subsides qui occasionnent des distorsions sur le marché agricole» (page 14 de l'Accord)? Les Américains ont déjà interprété, dans le cas du porc, que les subventions d'intérêts, la stabilisation des revenus et le programme R.O.P. constituaient des subventions.

Mais encore, l'Accord prévoit, à plusieurs endroits, que le Canada modulera sa position sur celle des Etats-Unis dans les négociations du GATT.

Si nous avons tort de nous inquiéter devant ces textes, il y a un moyen évident de rassurer et satisfaire les producteurs et productrices agricoles : que le traité soit clair et précis pour ne laisser place à aucune interprétation arbitraire ou circonstancielle. Dans un domaine aussi sensible que l'agriculture, aucune zone d'ombre ne doit persister surtout que c'est tout notre avenir qu'un tel traité engagerait.

Nous sommes en droit de nous poser une ature série de

184

■■■■■■■■■■■■■■■■■■■■■■■■■■■■■

questions. Pourquoi cette virulence à Ottawa et à Québec pour nous accuser de pratiquer de la désinformation? Pourquoi cette précipitation à déclarer haut et fort que l'Accord est bénéfique à l'agriculture?

C'est l'Union des producteurs agricoles qui doit réagir aux foudres conjuguées d'Ottawa et de Québec. Se pourrait-il que l'on veuille nous isoler? Nous sommes une cible propice car la vitalité de notre secteur est largement conditionnée, comme dans le monde entier, par l'intervention gouvernementale et l'on peut facilement ameuter le bon public en lui répétant que l'agriculture est hautement subventionnée et que, en cas de libre-échange, les prix des aliments *pourraient baisser*. Leurre et démagogie que tout cela!

L'agriculture n'est pas plus subventionnée que d'autres secteurs (automobile, entreprises, etc.) sauf que dans notre cas, cela se fait plus visiblement et par des programmes publics mais aussi, ce que l'on oublie de dire, par la participation financière des producteurs. Ensuite, prétendre que les prix baisseront, c'est faire abstraction d'une donnée primordiale : lorsqu'un marché devient captif, ce qui serait à moyen terme le cas ici sous la pression de la concurrence américaine, le vendeur décide tout seul de son prix. Pense-t-on honnêtement alors que les prix baisseraient à moyen et à long termes? A l'heure actuelle, pour certains produits américains circulant sans barrières et sans tarifs, les prix pratiqués ici sont pourtant plus élevés que les prix sur le marché américain.

Ce que l'on nous demande, c'est un autre acte de foi et d'espérance dans la capacité des négociateurs à défendre l'agriculture. Pourquoi serions-nous obligés de vivre de promesses après avoir été trompés? A moins que nos gouvernements aient trouvé là un moyen à revenir à des politiques ad hoc qu'ils affectionnent tant plutôt qu'à des interventions équitables et réfléchies.

Le libre-échange est un étouffoir qui produira ses effets à moyen et long termes mais que nous devons analyser maintenant. La naïveté des gouvernements peut-elle

185

vraiment expliquer à ce point leur méconnaissance de la réalité historique des relations commerciales avec les Etats-Unis?

Quant à nous, nous ne serons pas la grenouille dans la fable «La grenouille et le boeuf»!

"Canada today,

Mexico tomorrow . . ."

John Ralston Saul

John Ralston Saul, the author of three novels, of which the most recent is The Next Best Thing, *contributes regularly to* Le Monde *and to* The Spectator.

Throughout the free trade debate, we are constantly told that we must be competitive. That we can compete. But compete against whom?

The United States already has a virtual free trade pact with Mexico, or rather, with a strip of Mexico, several kilometres deep and running the full length of their 3,200-kilometre shared border. This official trade zone contains more than 1,000 American factories employing some 300,000 workers, mostly teenagers, non-unionized of course, and at wages of approximately 65 cents U.S. an hour. These "Maquiladora Industries" are expanding at a phenomenal rate. They constitute the second largest industry in Mexico. Second only to petroleum. Larger than tourism.

■■■■■■■■■■■■■■■■■■■■■■■■■■■■■■■■■

There is a second socially undeveloped industrial zone within the borders of the United States itself. Much of the American South, long an economic backwater, is devoting itself to a raw capitalism not unlike that of the late nineteenth century. American corporations have been moving their factories with great deliberation from the North to such states as Tennessee and Mississippi. Unions are technically possible in such places, but the state governments intervene to ensure that they are not practically realizable. Wages run at $6 to $7 an hour, approximately one-half those in the North, and industry operates in social and work conditions we have considered unacceptable for half a century.

The word ''competition'' is used enthusiastically by those in favour of North American economic integration as if there existed one universally accepted definition. In reality, each country understands something quite different by competition. And when intelligent agreements are struck to remove tariffs between countries, they are invariably based on a prior agreement over the nature of competition, in particular, over the standardization of social policy.

The key to Europe's success, for example, and the explanation for its slow evolution have been a determination to avoid destructive competition by first establishing similar social standards – length of work week, hourly wages, unemployment benefits, job protection, work conditions, medical, pension, and disability programs. This evolution has been consciously designed to force a raising of standards toward those of the most advanced countries, not a lowering toward the most backward.

No European nation could succeed in open competition against a Korea or a Thailand, which both maintain nineteenth-century labour conditions. The countries of the European Economic Community therefore limit that competition to their definition of the word by the use of regulations, which include tariffs. To do otherwise would be to lose an unequal combat and, in losing, to both subsidize and encourage an unjust system. To accept the

189

Asian definition of competition would be to destroy their own society.

The Canadian government, of its own free will, has committed us to precisely such an unacceptable and destructive definition. The Maquiladora Industrial Program was begun by the Mexican government in the 1960s. It was and is based on a simple rule: non-manufactured materials may be imported from the United States tax free, manufactured in Mexico, and re-exported tax free. The only government charge is an American value-added tax on the imported manufactured goods, a minor cost. By 1975 there were 450 plants; by 1986, one thousand. Approximately 50,000 new Mexican jobs are being created each year and the pace is constantly quickening. Most major American corporations are there – General Electric, RCA, General Motors, and so on. Japanese corporations are now looking with great interest.

The corporate pattern is to establish warehouses on American territory, in such places as El Paso, with two or three employees, then build factories on the other side. The original American intent was to concentrate on simple labour-intensive operations. They have discovered that modern industrial systems do not require the skills developed by high standards of education. They are therefore expanding the variety of their Mexican operations.

As for the Mexican government, it has encouraged this growth by devoting itself to industrial co-operation. Between 1971 and 1975 there were 482 worker appeals to the Mexican Board of Arbitration; 468 went in favour of the companies. Mexico City is now widening the program. In the future, 20 per cent of the manufactured goods may be sold tax free inside Mexico if some of the original elements are produced locally. In 1969, only 2 per cent of the manufactured goods imported by the United States came from Mexico. Now it is 40 per cent. Mexico, not Canada, is the largest exporter to America of manufactured goods. This growth indicates their "competitive advantage." It is against them that we must

190

■■■■■■■■■■■■■■■■■■■■■■■■■■■■■

win if we wish to pierce the American market for manufactured goods. But it is also against the Mexicans that we will have to win if we are to hold our own market, because Maquiladora goods count as American goods.

Why has Washington accepted this situation? A senator from Texas recently stated that "The progress of the Maquiladora plants keeps the U.S. competitive with the Far East." Implicit in these words is a belief that the social contract of the northern United States is too advanced. Exposure to open Third World competition from Mexico and the American South will continue to drain that contract until the middle-class consensus is broken. Of course, Canada has an even more developed social package, comparable to those found in Western Europe, Australia, and New Zealand. We are even less able to "compete" against nineteenth-century social structures.

The automotive industry demonstrates what is happening. General Motors now has seventeen plants in Mexico, with 24,000 workers. They plan to open another twelve Maquiladora factories and close another nine in the U.S., while looking for more complex Mexican investments. At a recent conference on the Maquiladora Industries, the president of Huron Plastics, a producer of automotive parts (1,585 employees, ten plants in Michigan), stated that the automakers "are moving to Mexico and they are putting it to us that if you want to do business with us you better move closer to us." Automotive parts manufacturers made up the biggest group of participants in the conference.

At the same meeting, Rex Maingot, president of American Industries, stated: "The bottom line is this. Your cost per Mexican worker is 69 cents per hour versus at least $9 in the United States – a saving of $15,000 per worker. You can see how down here a GM car can be made competitive with the Japanese. . . . If you are currently driving a Ford Tempo, there is a 50 per cent chance that your engine was built right here in Mexico. We project that

191

there will be one million more new jobs coming to Mexico from U.S. companies in the next fourteen years.''

Only naiveté or cupidity can have led our negotiators to accept indirect Mexican free trade without even addressing themselves to the Mexican and American governments on this question. Was it a desire to accept the Washington premise that the unleashing of unfettered Third World competition from Mexico and the American South would eventually reduce our production costs by undermining Canadian social programs, programs that no politician dares question openly? That certainly will be the effect. And, curiously enough, in refusing to negotiate social policies we have guaranteed that those of Mexico and Tennessee will become the norm. They, after all, will produce cheaper goods, thus ensuring that their unacceptable definition of ''competition'' will be the official North American version.

■■■■■■■■■■■■■■■■■■■■■■■■■■■■■■

"Significantly more women than men stood in opposition to the free trade agreement. And for good reason."

Laurell Ritchie

Laurell Ritchie is the executive vice-president of the Canadian Textile and Chemical Union, based in Brampton, Ont. She is also the first vice-president of the Confederation of Canadian Unions and a member of the employment committee of the National Action Committee on the Status of Women.

When the U.S.-Canada free trade talks began, many women assumed that the negotiations and the content of any potential agreement had nothing to do with them. What other conclusion could they come to when all the media headlines were about shakes and shingles, soft-wood lumber, and specialty steel? These are not jobs many women work at.

By the time public polls were conducted in the summer and fall of 1987, the results showed an obvious "gender gap" in response to free trade. Significantly more women than men stood in opposition to the free trade agreement.

And for good reason. Particular aspects of the proposed agreement would fundamentally alter women's employment, standard of living, and social position in Canada.

Women work in industries such as textiles, clothing, food-processing, electrical products, and other consumer goods, which are crucial to the industrial well-being of Canada. Textiles and clothing alone represent about 7 per cent of the national income and together are the largest industry employers in Canada. The food and beverage industries are the second largest employer, with the auto industry third. Any policy that threatens those industries would reverberate through the whole economy.

And the present deal does endanger them because tariffs and "non-tariff" barriers will be eliminated. While most Canadians understand the significance of tariffs, many do not appreciate the importance of other protective mechanisms, such as government purchasing policies that favour Canadian manufacturers. With the new agreement, Canadian clothing firms will no longer get preference when the Canadian armed forces, for example, buy new uniforms.

Then there is the service sector. About one-third of all women in the labour force work in clerical occupations; over 90 per cent work in service occupations. Yet there is little discussion about the impact of the free trade agreement on the service industry. What are they trying to hide?

The Americans want comprehensive free trade in services with Canada – something they have not achieved with any other country – because it will help reduce their immense trade deficit. They know that just about every type of service can be traded internationally, including banking, data-processing, insurance, telecommunications, computer services, air transportation, and culture.

I will give you only one example of the adverse effect on women's jobs in this open-ended free trade agreement. In data-processing, current restrictions in the Bank Act require processing and storing of data in Canada. If these

■■■■■■■■■■■■■■■■■■■■■■■■■■■■■■■■

restrictions were removed, and there is no indication that they will stay, many women's clerical jobs would be threatened as banks shift their data handling to low-wage areas of the United States.

When the federal government tells us that Canadians must "adjust" to the restructuring that will occur with free trade, what they are really telling us is that we must be prepared to accept smaller paycheques and poorer working conditions. A form of blackmail is taking place. If we don't accept these "competitive" conditions, we will lose our jobs.

Under stiff competition from large American firms in the same industry, many Canadian companies would fight much harder for concessions in union contracts and unilaterally reduce wages and benefits in unorganized workplaces. They would also intensify their efforts to erode or eliminate current provisions of employment standards legislation, minimum-wage laws, health and safety regulations, human rights laws, and other "government intervention" that threatens profit margins. They will do this because their major competition under the agreement will be located in states with no minimum wage, poor labour legislation, and very low levels of unionization. So they will head south if tariffs and non-tariff barriers are removed. Canadian workers will be held hostage to the demands of the companies.

The Canadian tradition of providing services to people through publicly supported systems and facilities is jeopardized by the free trade agreement, for it says that U.S. firms must be given equal treatment in Canada and cannot be disadvantaged in competition with public enterprises or other firms that receive public support. What this means is that U.S. firms may be able to claim equal access to public funding. The result will be a great drain on our tax dollars and an increased tendency for certain services in hospitals, schools, municipalities, child care, and so on to be shifted to the private sector. The nature of the delivery of social services is of great significance to

195

women. When services are delivered through private means, they tend to be less accessible and more expensive.

The federal government has dismissed the negative implications of free trade for women's employment, but it is quick to assert that women will make great gains as consumers. While the Consumers' Association of Canada has accepted the general hypothesis that prices will be lower because of cheaper imports under free trade, this organization finds itself doing battle against companion legislation that is a direct result of free trade. The most obvious example is its opposition to the drug patent legislation and the high prices that will ensue if the large U.S. drug firms monopolize drug production.

The very existence of domestic production provides price competition for any goods or services imported into Canada. If domestic competition is eroded or eliminated, importers will be able to charge virtually whatever they like for the things they sell. For example, when import restrictions on children's and men's shoes were eliminated in recent years, the result was not lower prices but a dramatic rise in cost. In the first fourteen months, 1,500 jobs were lost; at the same time, the price of imported children's shoes rose by 26 per cent and that of men's shoes by 7 per cent.

Since women's wages on average are only 64 per cent of those of men, women have a special sensitivity to the price of goods and services. The attempt to seduce women on this issue is irresponsible, and the argument itself has little basis in reality.

And the fate of half the people in Canada has been simply dismissed.

"... we have few bargaining chips left."

Abraham Rotstein

Abraham Rotstein is a professor of economics at the University of Toronto. He is the former editor of The Canadian Forum *and one of the founders of the Committee for an Independent Canada.*

The system of international trade under which we live, like much else in the international economy, is undergoing major changes. In the post-war period, we saw a concerted effort among the trading nations to reduce their tariffs and to open up their markets to each other. This great success in tariff reduction was achieved through the auspices of an international organization called GATT – the General Agreement on Tariffs and Trade. During many rounds of meetings in the post-war period, great advances in trade liberalization were made and all participating countries benefited substantially.

Canada, a country that had become accustomed to a

high tariff wall since Confederation, found that in this international forum it received many advantages, including easier access to the American market. Of course, we had to do our share. We "paid" for this improved access by lowering our own tariffs significantly.

The result at the end of the 1979 meetings (known as the Tokyo round) was a further gradual lowering of tariffs. By the end of 1987, 96 per cent of Canadian exports were slated for admission to the United States at a duty of 5 per cent or less. Considering the volatile level of currency fluctuations, 5 per cent is only a token duty. Indeed, at the present time, about 70 per cent of our exports are already admitted into the United States duty free.

But just at this juncture, when the tariff problem was on its way to being solved, a new impediment to international trade made its appearance, a so-called "second line of defence." This was a set of legal devices known as "injury clauses" and countervailing duties that made up a new system of non-tariff barriers. These devices formed the basis of court cases that were used by domestic firms to halt or slow up their foreign competitors. The broad aim was to create various roadblocks to slow down or otherwise relieve the pressure of foreign competition on domestic firms. A casual observer might have concluded that we were simply restoring the old tariff walls by the side door.

Canadians were particularly alarmed since the proportion of our trade that went to the United States had edged up to 78 per cent. Suddenly we went from a promising situation, where the traditional tariff barriers had largely been shunted aside, to one that was clouded with a new kind of uncertainty. No one could foresee when an American firm would bring a new action before an American trade tribunal that would result in a countervailing duty being imposed on Canadian exports to the United States.

The legal basis of most of the American complaints was that Canadian firms were "cheating," that is, that they

■■■■■■■■■■■■■■■■■■■■■■■■■■■■■■

were receiving "subsidies" from the Canadian government that permitted them to sell their products in the United States at an unduly low cost. The problem with that American argument was that there was no clear definition of what constituted a "subsidy." Indeed, much of what we in Canada regarded as regional development programs, or research grants or assistance to small business, might potentially be viewed by the Americans as a "subsidy" – except that no one could be sure until the action went through the American courts. Eventually, perhaps, a body of legal precedents would be established, but in the meantime a good deal of Canadian trade was clouded with uncertainty.

This situation provided the impetus for the Mulroney government's initiative for free trade discussions with the United States. While the traditional meaning of the term "free trade" had referred to the elimination of tariffs, we now stretched the definition to include exemption from the arbitrary and uncertain effects of the new American non-tariff barriers.

After sixteen months of negotiation, there emerged the "Canada-U.S. Free Trade Agreement." Every such agreement is necessarily a matter of give and take, the result of a rough-and-ready bargaining process. How are we to judge it? Let us try to draw up a rough balance sheet of what we gave up against what we received in return.

There are two main parts to the agreement. First, all remaining tariffs between the two countries would be eliminated over a ten-year period. The United States would benefit disproportionately here, since our remaining tariff wall is, on average, twice as high as that of the Americans. But that would be a relatively minor consideration if we were intent on phasing out the last of the tariffs between the two countries and thus to complete the process that had been sponsored by GATT in the post-war period.

But within this tariff agreement there is a major difficulty of another kind. This centres on the automobile

■■■■■■■■■■■■■■■■■■■■■■■■■■■■■■

agreement with the United States that traditionally guaranteed Canada its share of the automobile production for the North American market. The new draft agreement leaves this arrangement in limbo. It proposes a 50 per cent North American content rule for the automobile industry in North America. But it is not clear how Canada will be assured its share of that 50 per cent. Tariffs were previously an effective sanction that worked well for us in assuring that we got our share of the production of the North American market. This may no longer be the case. If it turns out, for example, that the American dollar drops in value in relation to other currencies – as it appears to be doing at the present time – then one of the advantages for American companies to produce in Canada will be gone. Without the 75-cent dollar, and without the previous sanctions based on the tariff, the future of our automobile industry would be in serious jeopardy.

Turning to the second part of the agreement, the area of non-tariff barriers, we had to give up a good deal more than we received. In the area of foreign investment, we agreed to relinquish the right to insist on certain performance criteria for foreign firms. We will, for investments below $150 million, no longer have the right to insist on provisions for local production, Canadian sourcing of parts and equipment, or other performance criteria. We will have to present an unqualified welcome mat for all foreign investment and to bind future governments to the same policies.

In addition, a continental energy pool will give Americans the right to acquire our oil, gas, and electricity on the same terms as if they were Canadians. We will be prevented from creating adequate reserves for our future domestic needs or from using energy to give us a special price advantage in any future industrial strategy.

Likewise, services, particularly financial services, will no longer be a protected sector. Americans will be able to buy into our banks and into related financial areas,

■■■■■■■■■■■■■■■■■■■■■■■■■■■■■■■

while Canadians will still be inhibited from equivalent concessions in the United States.

These are the main concessions that we shall have to make under the second part of this agreement. The Mulroney government assures us that no concessions were made in the area of regional development policy and cultural programs. But no indications have yet been given as to how we will be guaranteed exemption from U.S. countervail law in these areas.

Finally, let us look at what we receive in return for these various concessions. This is the most disappointing area of the whole agreement. We will have the right to participate on a joint tribunal with the Americans that will monitor American countervail decisions. But the scope of this tribunal will be very limited. Its restricted mandate will simply allow it to judge whether existing American countervail law has been properly applied. Decisions that are politicized or otherwise unfair can be reversed by the decisions of such a panel, but American courts, generally speaking, have applied American law in an objective manner. The main problem is not in the *distortion* of these laws but in the nature of these countervail laws themselves.

Under this agreement, the Americans still reserve the right to bring in new countervail laws as they see fit. Canadians, for example, will not be exempt from the new Omnibus Trade Bill, a very powerful protectionist bill now in the offing. Nor will the new agreement give us any relief on the previous rulings that have gone against us, such as the softwood lumber ruling, the shakes and shingles case, or the new tariffs on potash.

Down the road, say in five to seven years, the two countries will aim to work out a common code on countervail legislation. But at this last stage, we will already have made all the crucial concessions cited above and have few bargaining chips left. I suspect that what we will end up with is the American code on countervail, simply because the costs of cancelling the agreement at that point will be too great. The result is that we will have to retract most of the programs of regional and industrial development that are "countervailable," i.e., vulnerable because they are different from what the Americans consider legitimate initiatives.

I suspect that any objective observer would regard such a free trade agreement as decidedly unbalanced. What we are asked to give up seems quite out of proportion to what we will receive. In the end, our trade with the United States will hardly be more secure, while the pressure to conform to American rules and practices and to become a mini-version of American society will be enormous.

My own conclusion is that such a "free trade" agreement is a misnomer. We are just as hampered by the uncertainty of American countervail law. We are required in turn to give up a good deal of our economic sovereignty for the token benefit of reviewing the judgements of American courts relating to our trade.

It is as if, having paid the toll on the road to free trade once, we now find a second tollgate on the same road that we must pay to cross once again. But the toll is now much higher and the security offered to our trade is less. It is a very peculiar arrangement.

■■■■■■■■■■■■■■■■■■■■■■■■■■■■■■■
"Keep Canadian culture off the table – who's kidding who?"

Rick Salutin

Rick Salutin is a Toronto-based writer. His plays include
1837 *and* Les Canadiens. *He writes cultural criticism for*
This Magazine, *of which he is an editor, and is the author of*
Marginal Notes: Challenges to the Mainstream.

An exemption from free trade for Canadian culture, otherwise known as "keeping culture off the table," is not the issue. Even with current U.S. access, there's precious little left to exempt. Only 3 to 5 per cent of all theatrical screen time in Canada goes to Canadian films; 2 to 4 per cent of video cassette sales are Canadian titles; 97 per cent of profits from films shown in Canada go out of the country, 95 per cent to the U.S.; total prime-time broadcasting in drama and sitcoms is only 2 to 3 per cent Canadian; 95 per cent of English-language TV drama is non-Canadian; Canadian-owned publishers have only 20 per cent of the book market, though they publish 80 per cent

■■■■■■■■■■■■■■■■■■■■■■■■■■■■■■■■■■■

of Canadian titles; 77 per cent of magazines sold here are foreign; 85 per cent of record and tape sales are non-Canadian; in theatre, Canadian plays are the *alternative* theatre here; they are equivalent to off-Broadway, or off-off-Broadway, or London's Fringe. Keep Canadian culture off the table – who's kidding who? An end table, maybe.

We have a lot to be proud of among our writers and poets, our musicians and actors. But it's also true that we have barely a foothold in our own society. There is no comparable cultural situation anywhere. Our culture is not so much a reserve to be protected from free trade as a foretaste of its dangers.

The free trade deal, as we have it, does not exempt culture; it merely claims to. Elsewhere in the deal, postal advantages for Canadian magazines are scrapped, and recording and broadcasting are also affected. In fact, the exemption, as Michael Wilson has explained in the House, really applies only to open-investment policies.

Furthermore, in a truly sinister if obscure phrase, the U.S. is permitted to retaliate where it feels it has suffered "commercial" damage from Canadian cultural policies. There is far more to this than appears. The Canadian government, in this phrase, grants the legitimacy of American retaliation against measures we take to support and enhance our culture. We concede, more or less, that there is something wrong in taking such protective measures. We agree in advance not to fight retaliatory action by the Americans. Our regional and social policies are also under severe U.S. pressure, but only in culture has the government already completely conceded the validity of American counterattacks.

Note that U.S. retaliation is not restricted to the cultural area. If they feel commercially damaged by our cultural policies they may, for example, restrict entry to the U.S. of Canadian performers, but they may also retaliate in any other area: agriculture, resources, manufacturing – and we have given up in advance the right to object. Our

■■■■■■■■■■■■■■■■■■■■■■■■■■■■■

cultural support policies have effectively become hostage to the larger counters of commerce and trade. This is an exemption?

The *cultural* effect of this insidious phrase is to restrict the definition of culture that can be protected by the government to elite and minority forms. If we want to support the ballet, the opera, the symphony – *culcha* – the Americans will probably not object; those aren't part of their current market here. Not so with areas that enter the daily lives of most Canadians – publishing, TV, film, recorded music: if public policies aim to increase Canadian ownership and content in any of these areas and thereby decrease American control and profit, the Americans can claim that their interests have suffered, tote up the cost, and hammer us back in any way they want. If we want to avoid their retaliation we must restrict our cultural policies to those areas that have no commercial effects on American interests. The natural result will be a tendency to limit public support to the elite areas and to abdicate government action in the realms of mass and popular culture.

Much has been correctly said about how this agreement contains no definition of unjust subsidies and therefore leaves us exactly where we were. Supposedly there will be intense negotiations over definitions of subsidy during the next five to seven years. But there is one exception: culture. The agreement makes clear that any Canadian cultural policy costing the United States money is an unjust subsidy. Policies of subsidy for Canadian culture – except of the most elite and non-commercial sort – have already been acknowledged by the Mulroney government as illegitimate.

We have been told throughout the talks that the Tories were prepared to pacify the Americans with a "narrow definition" of culture; this is exactly what they have done, but in a way so subtle that as a writer one is tempted to admire it.

It would be extremely naive to think the Americans

207

■■■■■■■■■■■■■■■■■■■■■■■■■■■■■■■■

have been fought off in the culture wars. In fact, by winning the right to retaliate, they have already acquired a new weapon. It is folly to think they won't use it.

The entire history of our relations to the U.S. proves they take their cultural prerogatives in Canada most seriously, often more seriously than we take our own cultural rights here. The battle over *Time* Canada and *Reader's Digest* – to defrock them of "national" status and make a Canadian newsweekly possible – took decades. Since the Americans lost, ten years ago, they have not given up. They raise this issue again at every summit.

Or take the Canadian film industry. Let me peruse it since only the end of World War II. In 1947, the Canadian government prepared a policy to retain some of Hollywood's Canadian profits in Canada, for a Canadian film industry. Hollywood launched a massive campaign directed at ministers and officials, headed off the deal, substituted a lunatic program to insert Canadian place names in Hollywood movies, and nearly killed the National Film Board in the process. Every subsequent attempt to confront Hollywood's privileges here has met the same fate. As Secretary of State, John Roberts tried to introduce a film support program. The Americans mobilized. The program never happened. Francis Fox tried the same; he failed. The PQ government introduced a Quebec film distribution policy, Bill 109, which actually passed, but it was never implemented due to an intense and vindictive campaign by the American film industry. Now we have Flora MacDonald's extremely mild proposal on film distribution, which Jack Valenti of the American film industry calls a "viral contagion" threatening to engulf the world. MacDonald has not introduced the bill and will not introduce it; this has been reported as part of the deal. We know it is true for two good reasons: the U.S. affirms it, and the Canadian government denies it. And if MacDonald did introduce her bill, it would be subject to exactly the kind of retaliation we have granted as the Americans' right.

208

■■■■■■■■■■■■■■■■■■■■■■■■■■■■■■

The whole notion of an "exemption for cultural industries" is offensive, uncultured, and philistine. For suppose the government had succeeded in keeping culture off the table. As far as most writers are concerned, it would make no difference; we would still despise and oppose the deal. Artists I know were devastated by the announcement; one said she awoke next morning expecting to see American flags on the streets; pointing to an ostensible "exemption" for culture does not mollify us. Our feeling of national humiliation comes from our sense as Canadians, not as cultural specialists. It pains us to see our country put on the block; our energy resources handed out of our control and that of future generations; our ability to behave independently in the world curtailed. And as writers – what are we supposed to write our books about, and play our plays and sing our songs – when there is no distinctive Canadian society left; when our country has been absorbed into the glittering American marketplace – though I should amend that: the increasingly shabby American marketplace, visibly in decline at the very moment we choose to unite with it. Culture is not about culture, or literature, or art; it is about the way a people lives, in social and national groupings. What is the point of being a writer or artist in Canada, when Canada is no longer distinctive and in control of its destiny? The fight was never to save Canadian culture; it could only be to save Canada.

Our culture is already being severely affected by the free trade deal, and this has nothing to do with "exemptions" for cultural "industries." Our culture is not a matter of particular sectors or industries – dance, theatre, film, literature, sculpture, poetry, painting, video. All of these exist in a larger cultural context: the atmosphere in which we live, imagine, and express ourselves. The cultural air we breathe is already being invaded and poisoned by this deal. We are inundated with a new imagery. Michael Wilson says that deal opponents are "dominated by fear and weak of will." Donald Macdonald beats his

■■■■■■■■■■■■■■■■■■■■■■■■■■■■■■■■■

chest like Tarzan and howls, ''I don't see Canada as a sort of sheltered workshop for the inefficient, the incompetent or the less than capable.'' This imagery is Ramboesque and Nietzschean, full of taunts about cowardice and fear, the language of tough, lean, and mean, of winners and losers – and it comes to us from the America of Ronald Reagan. We're hearing this new kind of language everywhere from the proponents of free trade. It is the cultural atmosphere in which we, and especially younger Canadians, will increasingly be forced to formulate our thoughts. It is alien to most of us and our history. Of course, there is courage in the Canadian tradition, but it is not the courage of the ruthless and egotistical businessman; it is the courage of explorers and farmers facing a harsh landscape, and it has more often bred co-operation than competition. When we think of competition in a Canadian way, we tend to think more of hockey, and of teamwork, than of the American-style marketplace.

In this matter of culture, broadly and not narrowly understood, the free-traders reveal their true agenda. Most Canadians are perplexed when they look at the deal because they cannot see what we get for it; yet they assume the government must have something in mind. What they have in mind is their own, unannounced agenda: Reaganism, absorption into the ways, and means, of the American marketplace. For this reason it is clear why practically their sole organized support comes from businessmen (and women), who understand what is in the deal for them: a new kind of Canada, which looks exactly like the United States.

In the end, free trade is *entirely* a question of culture, because it is a matter of the kind of society we and our descendants will inhabit as a result of the deal. Culture cannot be exempt, and neither can Canada.

■■■■■■■■■■■■■■■■■■■■■■■■■
"Canada will be a less relaxed,
a less gentle, a less tolerant
place in which to live."

Denis Stairs

Denis Stairs is a professor of political science at Dalhousie University in Halifax, specializing in Canadian foreign policy. During the early 1980s he did research for the Royal Commission on Economic Union and Development Prospects for Canada, commonly referred to as the Macdonald Commission. Professor Stairs is the author of several papers on the free trade issue.

Politics thrives on mythologies. In the case of the politics of the free trade debate, two such mythologies are especially important to those who support the agreement. They should be unmasked by those who oppose it.

The first is that the proposed treaty with the United States is concerned with economics alone and has no other implication.

The second is that the significance of the treaty can be assessed solely by reference to the specific terms of the agreement itself. If, therefore, it poses any potential at

■■■■■■■■■■■■■■■■■■■■■■■■■■■■■■■■■■

all for secondary or tertiary effects on the way we live, or on the public policies by which we are governed, these will prove in practice to be trivial and hence can be ignored in responsible calculations of benefits and costs.

So deeply ingrained have these assumptions become that those who reject them in the interest of exploring the issue in its wider dimensions are commonly accused of "emotionalism" – as if, for example, the ancient question of the proper role of the state in society were a problem only for an irrational heart and not for a reasoning mind.

In fact, of course, the agreement will have enormous implications for Canadian public policy in a variety of fields, and these implications will become increasingly pervasive with the passage of time. This phenomenon – already in evidence – will come not so much from the specific provisions of the treaty document (although these will have an impact, too) as from the unleashing of political forces within our own society. Such forces will be difficult for governments to resist because the trade agreement will lend an almost irresistible legitimacy to their demands.

The immediate impetus for this process will be the effect of the treaty in establishing what the Americans like to describe as a "level playing field" – a field on which all the economic players are provided with approximately equivalent government advantages and are limited by approximately equivalent government constraints.

In effect, Canadian business enterprises will argue in Ottawa (and in provincial capitals, too) that while they have the courage and confidence to deal bravely with their American competitors in the continental marketplace, they can expect to be successful only if their costs of production, as influenced by government policy, are no greater than the corresponding costs of their counterparts in the United States. The logic of this argument, coming from industries that will be able to give persuasive evidence of competitive vulnerability on the one hand and enormous opportunity on the other, will be immensely powerful, and governments – provincial and federal alike – will find the practical implications difficult to deny.

What this means in concrete terms is that Canadian tax policy, and Canadian regulatory policies in a host of areas (product standards, labour codes, environmental regulations, and safety requirements, to name only a few), will all come under strong domestic pressure for ''harmonization'' with the equivalent policies in the United States. Since Canada is obviously the smaller and weaker player in the bilateral relationship, Canadian authorities can expect to do the bulk of the ''harmonizing,'' with the result that American patterns will define the limits of Canadian regulation.

In at least some areas of public policy, Canadians might conclude that the resulting amendments were improvements over current practice, although on this it is improbable that they would all agree. It is essentially for this reason that a few of the supporters of the treaty are willing to admit that it *will* have secondary effects on government behaviour – effects of which they will approve. From this point of view, the treaty is only partly about securing access to the American market and subjecting Canadian industries to the salutary cleansing of the cold shower. It is also about ''deregulating'' Canadian society – that is, about diminishing (after the American model) the role of the state in Canadian life.

Economists have an unhappy habit of regarding such matters as purely ''technical'' – bearing on no more than the issue of how the economy can be most efficiently managed. But the free trade agreement is not in this sense a politically neutral document. It contains a view of society – a laissez-faire view – which is central to what we normally regard as the crux of political argument and debate, and which, if accepted, will severely limit the range of choices, or policy options, that our governors will be prepared to consider.

■■■■■■■■■■■■■■■■■■■■■■■■■■■■■■■■

To illustrate, the government's recent proposals for tax reform, as well as its drug patent bill, are both examples of major initiatives of public policy that go to the heart of political life, in the sense that they are ultimately concerned with how the wealth of society is distributed. Certainly both measures have been debated to a large extent in these terms. But in each case the underlying impetus for the change – for the "harmonization" with American practice – has come from the requirements of the trading relationship with the United States. Once a treaty is firmly in place, Canadians will find this a recurring phenomenon, and one that will have surprisingly cumulative effects.

What this will mean over time is that Canadians will gradually find themselves subject to the assumptions and practices of a new "public philosophy" – a public philosophy that is well entrenched in the American tradition, but not in the Canadian. It is a public philosophy that tends, among other things, to identify the economic marketplace as the primary engine of society and of social policy. The contrast between the American and Canadian traditions on this matter is not, of course, absolute. The differences are differences of degree. But they are important differences nonetheless.

One way of illustrating them is to compare the attitudes of the two countries with regard to unemployment and the mobility of labour. With appropriate allowances being made for Congressional "log-rolling," through which American politicians (like politicians everywhere) seek to promote the economic interests of their respective constituencies in the hope of gaining electoral reward, the general operating assumption in the United States is that people should move to where the jobs are, rather than the other way round. If you are unemployed in Maine, you can solve your problem by moving to New York, or to Illinois, or to California.

In Canada, on the other hand, the corresponding assumption has always been that the application of this

215

principle of labour mobility must be softened by attempts to locate the jobs where the people are. Such attempts have been stimulated in part by the realities of electoral politics, but they have been sustained also by the conviction that economic efficiency is not the sole criterion upon which the quality of government should be measured. In this example, the preservation of our individual communities is seen to be a more important objective than a simple maximizing of the country's aggregate wealth.

Such policies reflect, in part, a public philosophy in which the harsh realities of economic competition are modified by a compassionate concern for the other ingredients upon which our well-being as individuals depends – a capacity to reside in the communities in which we have roots, and in which we are most comfortable and at ease, not being least among them. They also reflect the objective requirements of civilized living in an enormous country occupied by relatively few inhabitants, especially when most of these inhabitants are scattered in concentrations of varying size along a narrow corridor some 4,000 miles in length.

Supporters of the free trade agreement are naturally puzzled that such large concerns can be stimulated by what they see as no more than a technical instrument of good economic policy. The fact remains that the proposed treaty not only embodies but, if implemented, will further encourage a conception of government and society very different from the one that Canadians currently enjoy. Canada will be a less relaxed, a less gentle, a less tolerant place in which to live.

In contemplating the proposal before them, Canadians may wish to reflect on a melancholy observation by the philosopher, George Grant, in *Lament for a Nation* in 1965. "The kindest of all God's dispensations," he wrote, "is that individuals cannot predict the future in detail. Nevertheless, the formal end of Canada may be prefaced by a period during which the government of the United States has to resist the strong desire of English-speaking Canadians to be annexed."

"... the free trade deal promises few concrete advantages to fishermen, Acadians, or Maritimers in general."

Gilles Thériault and Rick Williams

Gilles Thériault is a social activist, an expert on fisheries development, and a well-known spokesman for Acadians in New Brunswick. For fifteen years he played a central role in the development of the Maritime Fishermen's Union. He currently is president of GTA Fisheries Consulting in Shediac, New Brunswick.
Rick Williams is an associate professor at the Maritime School of Social Work at Dalhousie University. He has written extensively on fisheries and regional development issues.

Behind all the rhetoric, the argument for free trade boils down to this: if sustained high mass consumption is the goal, the logic of the market demands greater economic integration with the U.S. All other choices about who we are as a society must follow from that bottom line.

In the Maritimes most people have made a choice already. If you want high mass consumption, go live somewhere else. If you want to live in your own way in your own place, stay. You pay a price to be a Maritimer, but most of us think it's worth it. In contemplating the free trade deal, other Canadians may want to reflect on this.

Fishing people epitomize this outlook. Fishing is an occupation that few people ever choose to take up. You have to be born into it with genes full of sea-knowledge, courage, and tolerance for cold misery. You have to want to live in places characterized as much by physical and cultural isolation as by their bleak beauty. A few fishermen earn big money, but most make just enough to stay at it and stay put.

We often hear the argument that there are too many fishermen in Atlantic Canada because of government programs like the Fishermen's Loan Board, boat subsidies, vessel insurance, and, most importantly, unemployment insurance. There are some in the Maritime business community who say that the only way to have a solid fishery is by a policy of survival of the fittest. That's how the Americans run their fishery. Everyone knows, however, that in terms of resource management our industry is much more developed than the U.S. fishery. The last thing we need is to base our fishery on their model. With free trade we may have no choice. The Americans won't change their system to ours.

Fishermen take the free trade issue seriously. Some 70 per cent of their product is sold through the Boston market. Due to poor management of their own fishery, U.S. fishermen cannot compete with Canadian imports. They blame the subsidies they feel Canadian fishermen get from government.

Tariffs are minimal in the U.S. fish trade, but the threat of countervail is a problem. Canadian policies have increasingly responded to American complaints about our social programs, regulated fishery, and regional development activities. Two recent International Trade Commission investigations have Canadian policy-makers actively considering, among other things, an end to unemployment insurance for fishermen. This would be devastating for an industry where average family incomes still hover around the poverty line. Thousands of fishermen would be driven out.

Under the current trade proposals the threat of countervail remains. There is no appeal until after the duties are imposed, and the fight is on their turf. The already serious U.S. interference in Canadian social and economic policies affecting the fishery will intensify in a free trade environment.

We will be better off if we keep our present management system (with improvements) and deal with the countervail threat as it comes. They need our fish, so we will always have a market. The long-term solution is to diversify our markets in order to have more bargaining power and to be better insulated against U.S. trade actions.

Perhaps the greatest danger in the free trade proposals is the reopening of the industry to foreign investment, or, in real terms: U.S. corporate takeover. The fishing industry on the East Coast is now almost entirely Canadian controlled. Our large corporations are among the biggest in the world, our medium-sized sized companies do very well, and we have a network of locally controlled cooperatives throughout the region.

Of course we've been through some hard times, and there will be more, but we have always survived in our own way. More than new capital, development in our fishery now depends on resource conservation, sound management, and market diversification. We are already twenty years ahead of the Americans in these tasks. Why would takeover by U.S. capital be a better way of dealing with such problems?

The lives of fishermen and plant workers are not easy. The work is hard and the rewards are uncertain at best. And, of course, there are the winters. But fishing people appreciate and like their lifestyle, even if they are always

looking for ways to improve it. They don't want to turn
it upside down. They don't want to do it the American
way. They want to do it their way.

In the Maritimes, Acadians have done it this way for
centuries. From their origins in the sixteenth century the
Acadian people were deeply committed to this place.
Long before any other European settlers, they had
learned to live in harmony with the rugged land and its
indigenous peoples. In 1755 their expulsion was com-
manded by land-hungry colonial administrators. Many
remained by retreating to the most remote areas of *Aca-
die*, while for generations *les expulsés* straggled back
from exile. Today the Acadians inhabit countless small
villages along the coast. Most still live by fishing, farming, and forestry.

By the 1950s and early 1960s, many Acadians had
come to believe that the way to improve their living standards was to learn to speak English. That was the way out.
Yet with the gradual influence of *la Révolution Tranquille*
in Quebec, the government of Ti Louis Robichaud in New
Brunswick, and the Acadian nationalist movement, more
and more Acadian flags were hoist up in front of multi-
coloured Acadian homes – not just to be flown on August
15th, the Acadian national holiday, but year round, even
during the harsh winter. Acadians came to understand that
the way to improve their situations was not to fit more
and more into the English way of life but to be more
affirmative about their own identity. They have flourished, and will continue to flourish, by understanding and
appreciating their roots. That is what makes them grow
in their own way, the Acadian way.

Acadians can't help but feel that this free trade business
is the same idea of ''let's do it their way – we will be
better off for it.'' They reply ''Jamais plus!'' Their language and culture survive and flourish when Acadians
take control of their own destinies. More recently, Acadians are learning to do it their own way economically.
Acadian-controlled businesses and co-operatives are

developing rapidly, especially in the fisheries. The American way is the melting pot, and perhaps it works for them. Canada is developing as a multicultural society. To succeed, we need more, not less, control over our economy. The Americans don't understand our aspirations and are not the least bit interested. But our way is not the timid way; our way is not the backward way. Our way is a different way and the only way for us.

In 1867 the Maritimes were enjoying their "Golden Age" of wood, wind, and sail. After Confederation, local investors moved quickly to take advantage of National Policy tariff barriers against American imports. By 1890 the Maritimes led Canada in the manufacture of steel, textiles, refined sugar, and other commodities. Maritimers had the capital, the skills, the competitiveness, and the head start. But once our economy was integrated *within* Canada, Maritimers were wiped out. By World War I the region had entered an economic slough from which it has never recovered. Why?

First, the rise of national monopolies drained capital from the region and flooded it with cheaper imports. Industrial giants such as Dosco and Dominion Textiles often bought out Maritime companies and then closed them to consolidate production and markets. Many local bankers and entrepreneurs played it safe and shifted their money to the centre. Then, as the central Canadian population grew, Maritime businesses found themselves chronically too far from the markets to attract investment, and without the political clout to win fair transportation policies.

Behind the National Policy tariff wall, Canada evolved as an industrialized core bracketed by poorer regions that exported raw materials and surplus population. Free trade *within* Canada certainly worked to encourage development of the most favoured regions, but in itself it did little to promote even development of the country as a whole. The antidote to regional disparities was the transfer of wealth from the centre through equalization, national social programs, and regional development initiatives. Without these there would have been complete economic collapse in the Maritimes.

This history reveals the underlying threat of free trade with the United States. The Maritimes' past is the Canadian future: larger U.S. corporations will swallow Canadian rivals, cheaper imports will close many local industries, production will move to the larger population centres to the south, and Canadian capital will follow it. The logic of the free market will make Canada a marginal society with a marginal economy. This time, however, there may not be a benevolent state willing and able to transfer wealth back to the new periphery.

In short, the free trade deal promises few concrete advantages to fishermen, Acadians, or Maritimers in general. As a basic economic direction for Canada, however, it represents a profound threat. We believe that greater economic integration with the U.S. will exacerbate regional disparities throughout Canada, and that the national capacity to counter such trends will be greatly reduced.

On a more basic level we reject the notion that our future should be determined solely by economic rationality. We need instead to decide who we are and how we want to live, and then shape an economy to serve those ends. Our history suggests that bad economic decisions result when human development is subordinated to market forces. The free trade agreement will not generate economic renewal in the Maritimes or reverse regional disparities, but it will jeopardize our cultures, minority languages, and ways of life – the things that make us who we are.

We hope that all Canadians, including those who may actually stand to gain in the narrow economic sense, will consider the full meaning of free trade. We hope that they will be willing to accept the challenges that fishermen, Acadians, and all Maritimers have long embraced to be ourselves in our own land.

■■■■■■■■■■■■■■■■■■■■■■■■■■■■
"From my perspective as an Albertan, it is incredibly important to Alberta and to Canada that this agreement be defeated."

Bruce W. Wilkinson

Bruce Wilkinson, a native of Saskatchewan, is a professor of economics at the University of Alberta in Edmonton, specializing in Canadian trade and commercial policy.

I am in favour of trade liberalization throughout the world, but I am very much against the economic integration agreement that has been negotiated with the U.S. It goes much beyond a simple free trade arrangement. Canada has surrendered its right in a number of areas to negotiate independent deals with third countries. It has also agreed to what is essentially a continental energy policy and to allow virtually unlimited and uncontrolled direct investment inflows from the U.S. to most industries, as well as fewer restrictions on personnel movements by companies. These are characteristics of a common market – which is even beyond a customs union in the degree of economic integration involved. If the current deal goes

■■■■■■■■■■■■■■■■■■■■■■■■■■■■■■■■■■

through, Canada and the U.S. will have a higher degree
of integration in many areas than exists within the European Common Market after thirty years! Yet, the ardent
supporters of negotiations with the U.S. said we were
only negotiating a free trade agreement.

The advocates of a bilateral agreement with the U.S.
have done Canadians a great disservice in several other
ways, too. They have repeatedly stated that the net
benefits from free trade would amount to 8 to 9 per cent
of GNP when in fact these benefits are more likely to be
only 1 or 2 per cent and could quite easily be negative,
given the error factors in the econometric models
involved, what we now know of the things Canada has
given up to reach an agreement, and the continued limitations that will exist on Canadian access to the U.S.
market.

They have also repeatedly told Canadians that never in
the history of the world has a free trade arrangement led
to political union. They have ignored that the Zollverein
was formed as a customs union in 1834 under the aggressive leadership of Prussia. In 1871 all the independent
nation-states in the Zollverein, except Luxembourg,
became a part of the nation known as Germany. They
have also ignored that Hawaii was once an independent
nation-state. It wanted assured access for its sugar in the
huge U.S. market, so it signed a free trade treaty with the
U.S. The U.S., to prevent Hawaii from negotiating a free
trade arrangement with any other nation, had the treaty
amended in 1887 so that Hawaii was not allowed to enter
into any other such agreements. It also prevented Hawaii
from allowing any other nation access to Pearl Harbor.
In 1892 a secret annexation club was organized in Hawaii
with the knowledge and tacit support of the U.S. administration. Finally, in 1898, after several machinations and
much debate, the U.S. unilaterally absorbed Hawaii without giving Hawaii so much as the right of a referendum.

The ardent supporters of free trade with the U.S. either
ignore the Hawaii precedent or dismiss it as being an

■■■■■■■■■■■■■■■■■■■■■■■■■■■■■■■

invalid representation of what the U.S. is like or might do today. I cannot accept that position. One only has to note that the U.S. has consistently refused to recognize Canadian sovereignty in the Arctic. The U.S. has also seen fit to ignore the traditional boundary between Alaska and the Yukon, the 141st meridian, when it extends into the Beaufort Sea, and has gone ahead to call for drilling licence applications for American firms in an area to the east of the 141st meridian. Finally, the U.S. wants to bend the dividing line between American and Canadian waters north of the Queen Charlotte Islands because that area happens to involve some of the richest salmon grounds on the Pacific Coast as well as possibly rich oil reserves. The U.S. is still an extremely nationalistic country.

The supporters of the current deal with the U.S. also seem to be trying to convince Canadians that the major objective Canada had in entering the negotiations – guaranteed access to the U.S. market – has been achieved when in fact it has not been. The arbitration panel that will be established to examine any dispute between Canada and the U.S. has no authority beyond checking whether the U.S. Department of Commerce has carefully followed U.S. laws, rules, and established administrative procedures. If the U.S. has done so, nothing more can be done by Canada, no matter how unfair from a Canadian perspective the decision of the U.S. seems to be. The battery of protectionist U.S. laws known as their contingency laws or "fair trade" laws have come through the negotiations unscathed. And if the new trade legislation being worked on by Congress at the moment becomes law, the protectionist nature of U.S. law will become even greater.

Suppose a Canadian company is accused of dumping products in the U.S. and that it has actually made ten separate sales in the U.S., five at prices above the Canadian price (which means that no dumping was involved) and five at prices below the Canadian price. U.S. law says that the Department of Commerce must look only at the five sales below Canadian price and on the basis of these find the margin of dumping involved and levy an anti-dumping duty accordingly. Again, many different factors may cause injury to an industry. Yet, according to U.S. law, in a dispute with Canada, if the Department of Commerce finds that even a *fraction* of the difficulty or injury that a U.S. company or industry is experiencing can be attributable to imports from Canada, then *all* of the injury to that industry must be attributed to the imports from Canada so that anti-dumping, countervailing, or other duties can be levied against the Canadian products.

We are told by our government that the agreement calls for new rules on subsidies and countervail to be agreed upon by the two parties over the next five to seven years and that if no mutually agreeable rules are achieved, one of the countries can abrogate the agreement. The fact is, however, that Canada has already given to the U.S. virtually everything that the U.S. wants, so we have little left to offer in return for the U.S. altering its laws or agreeing to changes regarding subsidies, etc. that Canada might want. Thus there is really no incentive for the U.S. to give up anything in this regard during the next seven years. If the agreement goes ahead, Canada will have become so integrated with the U.S. in seven years that there is no way it could afford to abrogate the agreement at that time. It would be locked in – and the U.S. knows it.

Many Canadians are not aware that even without any free trade arrangement about 80 per cent of Canadian exports to the U.S. already enter that market tariff free. Another 15 per cent face tariffs of 5 per cent or less, and only 5 per cent face tariffs above 5 per cent. These latter products are items such as clothing, textiles, footwear, and some petrochemicals.

Moreover, the Canadian dollar at seventy-five cents U.S. already makes a large proportion of Canadian products competitive in U.S. markets. If Canada were to cease its costly policy of keeping its interest rate structure one

■■■■■■■■■■■■■■■■■■■■■■■■■■■■■■■

or two percentage points above that in the U.S. it could lower the cost of capital to Canadian businesses, reduce the amount of Canadian borrowing abroad, and also lower the value of the Canadian dollar. If the Canadian dollar were only seventy cents U.S., Canada would gain about as much as having remaining U.S. tariffs removed and it would cost her nothing in terms of concessions to the U.S.

Here in Alberta where I live there seems to be a particularly exaggerated view of the benefits of the current agreement with the U.S. This view is expressed very strongly by both Premier Getty and the ex-Premier, Mr. Lougheed. The Premier has even suggested retaliation against anyone who disagrees with him. Usually when one resorts to using threats he is afraid his position is weak. Three of the major industries where gains are supposed to accrue are agriculture, petrochemicals, and the oil industry. Consider these in turn. The main gain in agriculture is expected to be increased exports for the pork and beef producers. If such exports occur, they may well be of a short-term nature only. American herds, for example, are at their lowest level since the early 1970s. With the excess of grains and other agricultural crops in the world today, much U.S. land has been taken out of production. It is not unreasonable to expect that if imports of meat from Canada begin to surge, much of this land would be diverted to pasture and feed grains, U.S. herds would be fairly rapidly rebuilt, and Canadian exports would be reduced once again.

Significant gains in petrochemicals could also be a short-term phenomenon. Canada has signed away the right to regulate or restrict exports of oil and gas to the U.S. If the U.S. in the future chose to import more gas and oil rather than petrochemicals, it would have the freedom to do this under the agreement and Alberta could do nothing about it. And in any event, Alberta will have to stop subsidizing its petrochemical industry via selling it natural gas at prices below the market price.

227

As for the oil industry itself, the hope is that the U.S. will now invest more in Alberta. The fact is, however, that the U.S. already knows that Canada is a much safer long-run source of supply of oil and gas than the Middle East. Hence, it already has a good incentive to invest in conventional drilling as well as oilsands development in Alberta. It does not need a free trade arrangement to cause it to do this. All the agreement means is that any new investment coming will be on American terms rather than on Alberta or Canadian terms.

Many Albertans, including government officials and politicians, seem to believe that the large oil service and supply sector that developed in the province after the Leduc No. 1 oil well in 1947 occurred naturally due to the working out of unhindered market forces. This, of course, is what the Americans would want us to believe. The fact is, however, that the Alberta government of that day had to enlist the support of the federal government to lean on the U.S. oil companies to buy more of their needs in Canada because they were bringing everything in from the U.S. The agreement that Canada has signed with the U.S. will ensure that in the future the Americans will be able to do this freely and Alberta will not be able to prevent them. To do so would violate the terms of the agreement, which Premier Getty says is so incredibly important to Alberta. From my perspective as an Albertan, it is incredibly important to Alberta and to Canada that this agreement be defeated.

What We Feel ■■■■■■■■■■■■■■■■■

The Lonely Land

A.J.M. SMITH

Cedar and jagged fir
uplift sharp barbs
against the gray
and cloud-piled sky;
and in the bay
blown spume and a
      windrift
and thin, bitter spray
snap
at the whirling sky;
and the pine trees
lean one way.

A wild duck calls
to her mate,
and the ragged
and passionate tones
stagger and fall,
and recover,
and stagger and fall,
on these stones –
are lost
in the lapping of water
on smooth, flat stones.

This is a beauty
of dissonance,
this resonance
of stony strand,
this smoky cry
curled over a black pine
like a broken
and wind-battered branch
when the wind
bends the tops of the pines
and curdles the sky
from the north.

This is the beauty
of strength
broken by strength
and still strong.

"Then suddenly, like a breeze hitting one's face, I think of Canada."

Daryl Duke

Daryl Duke is a film and television director of international reputation. His films Payday *and* The Silent Partner *have won distinguished awards, and his television series* The Thorn Birds *was one of the most popular series ever produced for American television. He is the founder and president of* CKVU *television in Vancouver.*

Late fall, near the mouth of the Pearl River in China. The engines of the boat we are on have suddenly been slowed, then stopped. There is a strange hush. No wind, no waves, no birds. And, incredibly for China, no other boats: no freight barges, no fishermen, no rowers ferrying river passengers with their bicycles from one shore to the next.

There is just heavy fog. Glassy river water. A world without motion.

We have been shooting for over a month. The heat, the humidity, the long hours, the constant script changes, the

231

■■■■■■■■■■■■■■■■■■■■■■■■■■■■■■■■

incredible and mounting problems of shooting in China have slowed each person. There is now no sightseeing on the daily river route to our location. Most sleep. One or two half-heartedly read yesterday's *Herald Tribune* or an old *Newsweek*. Some just stare, neither looking forward to the day ahead, nor dreading it. The day is just there. Another day to be got through on the long climb to finish the movie and go home.

I get up and climb the companionway to the pilot house. The five-man Chinese crew is gathered there. They are smoking and talking quietly, looking out at the dense fog. They laugh when they see me. They know no matter how the film company may rant, the gods who deliver fog upon the Pearl River have decreed our day's shooting will not begin on time.

I smile back at the crew. All of them think filmmakers are crazy. But they have got to know us. And now they are very paternal, even protective, about us and our strange needs and ways.

One crew member picks up a large thermos. I nod, then thank him in Chinese and take from him a cup of blisteringly strong tea.

I step outside the pilot house.

The boat sits alone in a grey dream. I hear the crew debate something behind me, their voices raised for a moment, then falling silent.

I look but see nothing through the fog. I know the rice fields are but two or three hundred feet away. That there are water buffalo nudging around the gates of the irrigation ditches. That on the water nearby a family – women, children, uncles, grandfathers, husbands, nieces – all will be living in the incredibly cramped cabin of some small freight barge full of stone, or coal, or scrap metal, or mountains of bamboo poles.

I hear a crew member clear his throat. Loud, uninhibited. A tremendous hawking sound. And then a noisy spit over the side and our realm of grey is silent once more.

232

■■■■■■■■■■■■■■■■■■■■■■■■■■■■■■■■

China. I am in China, all right.

Then suddenly, like a breeze hitting one's face, I think of Canada.

Fifteen hours back through time. In Vancouver it is still yesterday. Three in the afternoon. People are still shopping, banking, taking coffee breaks. On the Lions Gate Bridge, the rush hour hasn't begun.

In Toronto evening is coming on. Dinners are just being cooked. Knowlton Nash hasn't done his news yet. Yesterday. In Canada it is yesterday.

I think of Vancouver sitting at the end of time. The wet November air filling the cedars, the winter underbrush still and dying, molecule by molecule. I think of those endless inlets of the British Columbia coast, without people on their shores, or vessels upon their waters. I think of my mother up that coast when she was young, pinning magazine pictures of John Barrymore and Clark Gable on the walls of a rough wooden cabin by the sea. I think of the exiles, of the immigrants, and of the slow filling up of those empty forests.

I hear the noise of an engine. I am back in China. The fog is separating, opening above to blue sky, and astern to another one of the boats the film company has chartered. This one is larger than the one we are on. This one carries extras for today's crowd scenes. Dozens and dozens of members of the Chinese Army. All young men. Teenagers really. At the location they will be put in 1830s wardrobe. Now they hang out of every space laughing, smoking, calling out to one another. Their boat slowly glides up beside us.

The skipper of our boat comes out beside me. He shouts to the other crew. There is an excitable, rather heated discussion of which I understand not a word.

My thoughts of Canada are torn from my mind. Our engines start up again. I am back in the job. Back in the today of China. On the Pearl River. A long way from home.

. . .

■■■■■■■■■■■■■■■■■■■■■■■■■■■■■■

They say the beginning of mental health is to know who you are and where you are. I wonder how far for any of us that knowledge has progressed? And how far with such knowledge has this country, Canada, progressed?

Gabriel Garcia Marquez wrote in *The Solitude of Latin America*: ''The interpretation of our reality through patterns not our own serves only to make us ever more unknown, ever less free, ever more solitary.'' I read these words and think of Canada, struggling still to be born. Struggling perhaps more than ever to breathe in an atmosphere perhaps more than ever not its own.

This I do know. Ownership is programming. If free trade changes the ownership of Canada then free trade will change how we speak to one another and what we know of ourselves. In the end the hand that holds the shares holds the pen, the camera, the printing press, and the TV station.

Today, before free trade, how few films are made about who and what we are. And how few get distributed and shown in theatres of our own. How few TV shows speak of anything of substance. The CBC gropes for a philosophy like a blind beggar with a tin cup. The NFB is voiceless across the land. And our private broadcasters, those balletomanes of the bottom line, have for a generation made their yearly buying trips to Los Angeles, filling their TV schedules to the very maximum with the outpourings of Columbia Pictures, Paramount, Lorimar, Screen Gems, Universal. And this before the carte blanche of free trade.

Ownership is programming. Behind the boardroom door, does anyone worry about ''patterns not our own''?

I return each time to Canada sensing how fragile is the knowledge we have of ourselves. In how few hands that knowledge lies. How slender the opportunity to speak. Who are we? Will anyone ever know? In the end will there be anyone to care? . . .

This notion of Canada. How would I set it down for my

234

sons? Or leave it in a bottle flung in the sea? Or in a capsule tumbling through the darkness of space?

For each of us what an indistinct scenario. For my sons I could but piece together a few stories told to me as a child before the illness of relatives, divorce, and time itself scattered the family and I looked around to find all the elderly gone. But for a few fragments the book of dreams and struggle was closed.

Chance brought their first relatives, my great-grand-parents, to Canada. They were Quakers and in the mid-nineteenth century they found it was more than time to get out of England. They landed on the docks of Montreal and turned around to find all their luggage – their heir-looms, paintings, furniture, everything – had been stolen.

Later, it was chance as well which moved the family west from the farms of southern Ontario. A great uncle spurned in love as a young man took the new railroad to British Columbia. By the turn of the century all his brothers had joined him. As a family they were educated, interesting, passionate. And all nearly unemployable. Especially in Vancouver still pulling stumps and clearing land for houses. One was an amateur astronomer. He went to Hawaii, met Jack London and Queen Liliukalani. I think he could have happily spent the rest of his life in the tropics. Another wrote nature stories for children and spent his days collecting insects and endlessly detailing the flora and fauna of the coast.

So many stories. My mother yearning to become an actress. Succeeding and playing Desdemona and Ophe-lia. But seldom with a cent of income. And my uncle playing Othello and Richard II, having to write musical reviews in order to get free tickets to operas and plays touring through early Vancouver.

How to bring alive for my sons a Canada before the CBC, the National Film Board, the Canada Council, Tele-film? Before any support for the arts? A Canada more than simply a picture of the Queen on the post office wall?

■■■■■■■■■■■■■■■■■■■■■■■■■■■■■■■

How to tell them we long ago opted for a Canada that was distinct and not for sale?

The modern Japanese poet Okamota Jun wrote:

And on the battlefield
Of quiet dreams,
Amid the swirling cannon smoke,
A tiny gentleness,
A flower that does not wither.

For any of us in the arts it seems the battlefield has not changed. We work to protect the quiet dreams of those who went before us and today especially those who shall come after.

"We go forward, facing back."

John Gray

John Gray, winner of a Governor General's Award for drama, is a Vancouver-based writer/composer and the author of Billy Bishop Goes to War, Don Messer's Jubilee, Eighteen Wheels, *and* Rock and Roll.

Canada's national tree is the maple. Its animal is the beaver. Its sport is hockey. Its folk hero is the Mountie. Its musical instrument is the fiddle. Its gun is the shotgun. Its appliance is the heater.

Some people think Canada's vehicle is the train, or perhaps the snowmobile, but really it's the rowboat. We go forward, facing back. We can't see where we want to go, but we can see where we don't want to go. Except for the native peoples, Canadians live here because somebody didn't want to live someplace else. When we vote, we vote against the politicians we don't like.

We can see what we want to avoid, so we're sceptical,

■■■■■■■■■■■■■■■■■■■■■■■■■■■■■■■

but we can also see where we've been, so we're able to gauge our direction without seeing it exactly. But still we're nervous. We'd be a lot happier if we could see exactly where we're going; imagining it has become our national dream.

Our boat is on a fast river, and the river is flowing into a big lake. We're not in the lake yet, but we're close enough that we can see the dead fish and the McDonald's wrappers. It's too polluted. The food chain is top-heavy from too many predators. We don't want to go there. We never have.

If we are to avoid that lake, we have to head upstream, which isn't as easy as heading downstream but it builds up muscles, and we've been doing it for a while now so we're quite strong really.

To negotiate the rapids we have a left oar and a right oar. Sometimes we favour the left oar, sometimes the right, according to whatever it is we want to avoid. These shifts are subtle and short-term: we know that should we favour one oar too much, the rowboat will go around in circles and we'll simply drift downstream.

We want to continue forward because we believe that, somewhere upstream, there is a lake that is unlike the lake downstream: a pretty, clean, ecologically balanced lake where predators are under control. We're trying to get there, even though it means going against the current.

Our rowboat is guided by a series of Navigators who are never entirely trustworthy. As long as they can convince us that they know where our boat is going, they get to keep that comfy, important seat at the bow while we do the rowing. They want to remain Navigators for as long as possible. So when they're confused, they have every reason to pretend they aren't.

A confused Navigator traditionally misleads us in one of two ways. One technique is to describe the lake we want as though it were just up ahead, when in fact the Navigator can't see a thing. This sham has been maintained for as many as twenty-five years. Whole genera-

▪▪▪▪▪▪▪▪▪▪▪▪▪▪▪▪▪▪▪▪▪▪▪▪▪▪▪▪▪▪

tions of Canadians have rowed furiously into the murk, thinking that any minute they'll be skimming across that shining clear water. But sooner or later we realize we've been fooled. When that happens, we get another Navigator.

When the new Navigator becomes confused (most of them do), he can't use that technique because we've heard it before, so he resorts to another one: he points in the opposite direction, downstream, and shouts: "Forward!"

"But that's not forward!" we protest, gritting our teeth and rolling our eyes. "That's exactly where we *don't* want to go!"

"Nonsense," dissembles the Navigator. "In fact, you've always wanted to go that way in your heart. That direction is a lot easier. Those dead fish and styrofoam cups? Pay them no notice. Our boat won't be affected by that. I've negotiated a space for our boat in the lake that will be entirely free of styrofoam cups and teaming with fish at tremendous savings. The water in that spot will be as pure as any lake you might ever have found upstream. And the crocodiles will be under control: if they chew our boat, there will be a full review. Don't be so negative. You're heading upstream because you're afraid to face the real world."

"We don't believe any of that!" we reply, although how we wish some of it were true. "We're not going to listen to you! We've got eyes! We can see in the same direction as you can, and besides, it's our boat!"

"You're getting emotional," replies the Navigator. "I'm the Navigator and I say turn around, so turn around, dammit! Ah! I can see just upstream where we're headed, and it's terrible! Rocks! Big, horrible rocks that will tear our boat to pieces! Emergency! Hard right! Hard right!"

"No!" reply some rowers. "Yes!" reply others.

The rowers become frenzied and confused. Canadians who think there is something downstream for them pull the right oar, while Canadians who don't pull the left oar, and everyone knows what happens when rowers don't pull together. The boat just kind of slops around, goes nowhere, and . . . drifts. So we go through a dreary period of slopping around, going nowhere, drifting downstream like a hollow twig.

Then we get another Navigator. About time, too.

There is a lake up there, my Child. Keep rowing against the current. And watch the Navigator.

". . . a blot on the map . . ."

Laurier LaPierre

Laurier LaPierre has been a professor of history at McGill University in Montreal, a contributor to many Canadian journals and newspapers, and a host of the CBC's This Hour Has Seven Days. *He is now a broadcaster for CKVU television in Vancouver, and his historical account of the conquest of Quebec in 1759 will be published next fall. He lives in Britannia Beach, B.C., with three dogs and a cat.*

To Michael,
In a Federal Penitentiary,
Somewhere in Canada

Dear Michael:
You have asked me why I am so agitated about this free trade deal between Canada and the United States. "After all," you said, "Canada is just a blot on the map and it will always be there."

It's quite a blot, you know. It occupies four million

square miles of the surface of the planet. It is the second largest country in the world, stretching as it does over half a continent.

I know, of course, that it can be obliterated by nuclear bombs. It can be destroyed by pollution and the raping of the land. And it can be devastated by the greed and decay of those living on it. But should not all our efforts tend to prevent such disasters and make us worthy of what has been handed down to us? I think so. And so do you in your heart.

No, Michael, Canada is not just a blot on the map. It is a country. It is a land. It is the sum total of our will-ingness to live in Canada and to be of it in order to build a society which is just and sane and capable of making a distinct contribution to the peaceful evolution of man-kind. And from time to time to do great things together! That is what a country is.

Canada is not a commodity to be bargained away to the highest bidder in the marketplace. This is essentially why I object to the agreement before us – an agreement which has been arrived at in secret. This is my country. This is your country. It is all we have. I give no one the right to sell it. I give no one the responsibility to weaken it. And I sure as hell am not going to give anyone the opportunity to harm it behind my back.

I suppose you are asking me why I care so much. I will tell you.

Canada has made all what we are. Oh, we have not always responded to its challenges with sanity and justice. But when we lived in harmony with the land, we became more united, more creative, and we gave a little here, a little there, to be together. That is important.

Above all, we survived with a degree of equality. It has cost us dearly, but we did it – and we should be proud of that. We forged a unity in diversity, allowing the space to take us all in. We adapted political institutions and systems that sought to reconcile the differences imposed by the mix of our people, the lay of the land, and our

■■■■■■■■■■■■■■■■■■■■■■■■■■■■■

concept of liberty. To overcome the difficulties inherent in our geography, we built a mixed economy founded on the principle of equal and just distribution of the wealth produced by our labour. And we gave ourselves strong laws to protect our way of life, our environment, our culture, and our social fabric.

We did all that as we cleared the land, conquered the wilderness, filled the space, harnessed the rivers, and built our cities, our villages, and our community life. In the process we became a distinct people with our own ways of looking at and doing things, with a cultural identity that speaks of us, and with a profound sense of belonging to the land and to the planet Earth.

I want this to continue.

Then there is the beauty of it all! The deep coves of Newfoundland; the rolling sand dunes of Prince Edward Island; the strong earth of Acadia; the gentle hills of Gaspé softening the modernity of central Canada; the flowing majesty of the St. Lawrence coming from the very depth of the five mighty seas that men call lakes; the fearsome pre-Cambrian shield that dominates us all; the endless Prairies with their horizon lost in the gold of wheat; the towering mountains that shelter the land of the Pacific; and the endless North that beckons us to eternity. I don't want to lose any of it.

Our people have always known in their hearts that there was a price to be paid to be Canadian. Often the lure of the south has been powerful. It would be so much easier to give in; but we would lose ourselves in the shuffle. We have always felt that and that is why we have resisted the continental pull. We must do it again.

Much love,
Laurier.

■ ■

"Once upon a time there was a country called Canada."

Jack McClelland

Jack McClelland is identified with Canadian publishing and is single-handedly responsible for the cultivation of Canadian writing in the past thirty years. He lives in Toronto.

Once upon a time there was a country called Canada. Fair enough, kids, I don't tell you fairytales and I don't talk to you that way, but I have asked you about free trade with the U.S.A. and you don't really know about it. They are not talking about it yet at your school. But I would first like you to know about it.

First, I would like you to know the fundamental difference between the U.S.A. and Canada. Speaking historically, in the U.S.A. the rights of the individual are the single most important belief. In Canada, we believe in the rights of all people. The rights of the individual are less important in Canada than the rights of all Canadians. It is that simple. In your classroom, the rights of the whole class are more important than your rights. In the U.S.A., the individual who wants to disrupt the class for whatever reason – well, that is part of American belief, faith, and constitution.

You don't know what free trade means. In all truth, neither do I. The details remain a very closely guarded secret. Let me give you an example of my worries about free trade. In Florida and in a number of other states in the U.S.A. it is permissible to carry a handgun in order to protect yourself in case somebody attacks you. This is called the right of the individual. To protect yourself you can shoot first. I suppose that is fair enough if you believe that much in the rights of the individual. In Canada, as yet, we have neither the right nor the need to carry such weapons (although crime is hardly absent from our streets), but the very secret nature of the so-called free trade agreement makes me wonder if handguns will suddenly be available to every Canadian who wants to carry a gun.

Kids, let's start. Once upon a time there was a country called Canada. Not only was it a land of indescribable beauty from its Atlantic coastline to its Pacific shores, it was a land so richly endowed in natural resources – precious and industrial minerals, oil, gas, fresh water, trees, rich sod – a land so richly endowed as to be unrivalled anywhere in the world.

It was not an exaggeration to describe the inhabitants of this country as the most advantaged people in the world – a relatively small group considering the great land mass that was our heritage, and the people sat on top of the richest storehouse known to man.

This land was originally owned by Indians and Eskimos. It was stolen from them by the French. Then it was stolen from the French by the British. Finally it became an independent nation, proud at long last to be in charge of its own destiny. That very brief account of Canada's history gives no detail of the toil, hardship, bloodshed, anguish that went into the creation of this proud and inde-

pendent country. But the details are available everywhere. We have been fortunate in our natural inheritance;
we have been more than fortunate in our gifted authors
who have told us about our past, our present, and our
future. I plead with you to read Frederick Philip Grove,
Gabrielle Roy, Margaret Laurence, Stephen Leacock,
and so many others. They will give you some feeling
about our great country.

That story of a people and a land is invariably true in
recorded history: a harsh mixture of human self-sacrifice
and greed. We have had our share of national heroes, and
we have had more than our share of national rogues who
for the worst sort of greed would sell our heritage or even
their own grandmothers to seek some advantage.

The latest rogue may indeed become the most infamous
in our history. We elected this smiling, genial man as our
eighteenth Prime Minister. Without direction from us or
any prior warning, he has done a two-step dance that may
well destroy our heritage.

The first step, called a Meech Lake Accord, was
designed to weaken any central control in Canada. His
second step was, in reality, a blank cheque to our American neighbours to turn Canada into an annex, a ware-
house, a storehouse of riches that they could call on in
the future.

Kids, this is not the story about the wicked grand-
mother. I have dropped all that. But it is the story of a
wicked Prime Minister who has sacrificed your heritage
for reasons that I don't at the moment understand and I
don't think I will ever understand. He said the move is
to protect us from U.S. greed and self-interest. Nonsense,
I say to you. There is nothing new or particularly threatening about U.S. greed and self-interest. It has always
existed. They are great people, good neighbours, and I
love them, but I don't want your heritage to be given up
for them.

To become a citizen of the U.S.A., all a Canadian has
to do is cross the border and fill out a few forms. It is not

■■■■■■■■■■■■■■■■■■■■■■■■■■■■

very difficult and hundreds of thousands of Canadians have already done it. I don't know of anyone who is unhappy about that decision. I recommend it to our Prime Minister. I think he should cross the border, fill out the forms, and become a U.S. citizen, but I plead with him not to take me or you, my grandchildren, or our country with him. Let's just leave us alone. We will find a new Prime Minister, in time. But, please, can I deliver my heritage to my grandchildren and let them decide their own future?

"My questioning . . . is not a defence of the status quo."

The Very Rev. Dr. Lois M. Wilson

Lois Wilson, former moderator of the United Church of Canada, is co-director of the Ecumenical Forum of Canada and one of seven presidents of the World Council of Churches. She has four children, five grandchildren; the eldest grandchild is named Nora.

So, Nora, you want to know what I think about the free trade agreement. It's very like ham and eggs, but you'll have to wait a bit for me to explain that.

Do you remember that time we spent in Minneapolis with the Ingelin family, and the night we spent talking about what makes Canadians different from Americans (other than the fact that we end our sentences with "eh?" and they end theirs with "huh?")? Remember how we concluded that people in both countries speak English, but that doesn't necessarily mean we speak the same language? Nice people, the Ingelins. Our disagreement is not about liking Americans. It's about our distinctiveness and about wanting to be who we are. Our history, our economic, social, and cultural needs, our way of doing things, and our role in the world are so different from those of the U.S.A.

I think Canada is a distinctive, unique country. We're not California and New York. We're Thunder Bay and Nelson and Truro and Corner Brook and Lachine. We don't want to be a melting pot. We want to nurture and celebrate our distinctiveness in the world of nations, and our pluralism internally. We have developed our own distinctive institutions and ways of doing things. Most Canadians, including supporters of free trade, agree that our government must intervene sometimes to promote just, sustainable, and participatory economic policies. So you should be alert to the possibilities of the ways a free trade agreement might tie the hands of our government to do this and make us less flexible in our political life.

A free trade agreement, which would be mainly about economic matters, would have enormously important ramifications for Canada in social, political, and cultural areas as well. Don't get me wrong. My questioning of the free trade deal is not a defence of the status quo. We certainly need some changes and new approaches to economic issues. But it is important that we don't simply turn ourselves over to the control of our neighbours to the south and become politically dependent on them.

You see, Nora, one cannot divide economics from the other parts of the life of a society. To have free trade in economic matters might well encourage cultural, social, and political integration with the U.S.A. in the long run. I hope we don't close down our options in that way. I want a Canadian future for you.

My understanding is that free trade means government should interfere neither to restrict nor to encourage trade between Canada and the U.S.A. Let the market forces of supply and demand and the competitiveness of the marketplace shape our trade relationships. At first glance, it sounds fine. We would have the possibility of more markets and more wealth, which is supposed to bring more happiness. (You know me well enough to know I don't buy *that* assumption!)

But for whom? For the poor, the native peoples, the women, the marginalized, the hungry? I think not.

In the first instance, some few Canadian entrepreneurs might in fact hustle and cut out their competitors, and make a bundle for themselves. But it would be for themselves. I'm unwilling to allow market relationships and forces determine human relationships in this country. Some of us value the ways in which our governments have managed to develop public and social programs over the years. It's been important to care for those on the bottom of the heap, and to make some basic services available to everyone. It's one of the features of Canadian life that foreigners envy. And for you, Nora, a basic teaching of your faith community. And Canada has managed to do some of this, even though imperfectly.

In Canada we have become accustomed to a certain amount of benign government intervention in the economy, to assure citizens of adequate health care through medicare. Canadians are justifiably proud of services such as medicare. High-quality medical service is available to all, while health expenditures in Canada are much lower than in the U.S.A. We spend approximately 8.5 per cent of our GNP on health care to provide universal medical coverage, while Americans spend 10.5 per cent of their GNP to provide only partial health care to some citizens. And I don't have to take time to advise you, Nora, to never take sick when in the U.S.A., as you remember what happened to Uncle Jack and the enormously high medical bills he piled up.

Canada has a number of public and social programs that are a safety net for Canadians, and which have widespread acceptance in this country. It is, of course, highly unlikely that Americans would explicitly ask that these social assistance programs be dismantled. But Canada's

■■■■■■■■■■■■■■■■■■■■■■■■■■■

generous social programs, such as unemployment benefits, hospital insurance, baby bonus, and day-care services, could be under market pressure to be reduced or
eliminated. Of course, this isn't certain, but it's one of
the unknown but probable consequences of a free trade
agreement. We've seen social programs cut in some provinces of this country, when free trade mentality has been
in the ascendancy.

In some ways, Canada's agreement for free trade
would be making "a preferential option for the rich"
rather than "for the poor," which is the focus of our faith
commitment. And don't get sucked into believing that the
"trickle-down" theory works. You know how it is supposed to work. Let's get the money made, and *then* we'll
think about its distribution to the aged, poor, and disadvantaged. I don't buy that and I hope you don't either.
Let's talk about social programs *before* we lock ourselves
into a free trade deal that will disadvantage the poor even
more than the present system.

Nora, have you thought about what the free trade agreement may mean for women? Most of us (over 80 per cent)
are employed in service industries such as retailing, res-
taurants, hotels, financial services, clerical work, and
information processing. Up to 7 per cent of the labour
force would need to "adjust," which is a sophisticated
word for losing your job. That is, workers would need
to shift employment from one sector to another. Women
in the service sectors are not that easily retrained or relo-
cated because in these sectors they tend to be older than
the average female worker. They are much more likely
to be immigrants who cannot easily speak English or
French; they are likely to be married, and therefore are
not easily mobile; and they tend to have considerably
lower levels of education than the average female worker
in Canada. So women in the service industries will feel
the full negative force of the free trade agreement. All
this for fairly meagre access to U.S. markets.

One of the problems, Nora, is that Canada is so small

in comparison to its giant neighbour to the south. We have so much at stake here, including our own identity as a nation. You see, we are still struggling to create and preserve a distinctive cultural identity. We want to affirm the emerging distinctiveness of our culture by writing and publishing magazines reflecting Canadian realities. We want to develop our own films and records, reflecting the regions of Canada to each other and to the world. And because we are only 25 million people (not a large market for Canadian magazines or records), we have needed postal rates for over 260 Canadian magazines to be lower than those for American magazines. It's to give us a little breathing space until we are firm in our own identity. The free trade agreement proposes to *remove* these supports to Canadian magazines. I think it's too high a price to pay. If we pay it, you will have to entertain your children with stories of what you remember of a country called Canada that existed when you were a little girl.

The main problem I have with free trade, Nora, is that we have a great deal to lose because we're small. But the proposed partner, being so big, can bully us into concessions that aren't really all that important to it, but are our very life blood. Our very identity as a nation is at stake in this deal. It reminds me of the story of the pig and the hen talking about ham and eggs.

"For you," said the pig, "it's only another egg. But for me, it's my whole life."

And that's what I think about free trade.

"Déjà-vu!"

Farley Mowat

Farley Mowat is one of Canada's great storytellers. Twenty million copies of his books – particularly those on Canada's North – have been published in many languages around the world. His best-selling work, Never Cry Wolf, *has been made into a major motion picture. Controversial and pungent, Farley Mowat is not allowed into the United States.*

I come honestly by my propensity for shouting alarms into the night. I am a *Canadian*, not a surrogate Yank pretending to be Canadian as are all too many of our political and business leaders. On my mother's side I am descended from a Huguenot stonemason, Sebastian Hodiau, and his wife Urbaine, who arrived on the banks of the St. Lawrence River in 1645, and whose progeny, well fortified by admixtures of native blood from the true First People of the continent, fought, and some of them died, repelling the American invasion of Lower Canada in the infamous War of 1812.

My paternal ancestor in Canada, Sgt. John Mowat, helped chase the Americans back across the Niagara River after their attempt to seize Upper Canada during that same war. Oliver Mowat, one of the sergeant's sons, became the first premier of Ontario and a Father of Confederation. Oliver was my great great uncle. In one of his letters, written to a nephew near the end of his life, Oliver penned these prophetic words:

"They [the Americans] will never disabuse themselves of their conviction that Canada is rightfully theirs to do with as they please. It can only be by the exercise of the utmost vigilance and determination on our part that their attempts may be frustrated. . . . There are those in our midst who, while pretending to be patriots, will do all within their power to suborne our desire to remain free to pursue our own destiny and to maintain this Nation."

Déjà-vu . . . déjà-vu!

October 21, 1987. Thanks to my publisher's munificence, I am sitting in the first-class cabin of a plane bound from Calgary to Toronto intent on finding out what the Americans are thinking about free trade. On my left sits a large, dominant, but friendly fellow who volunteers that he is the executive "troubleshooter" for a gargantuan U.S. corporation that controls a large part of Canadian gas and oil reserves. He's delighted to talk about "the free trade deal" and, as he extols its virtues, he is joined (as by a Greek chorus) by passengers across the aisle and behind and in front of me. Because they are all large and imposing, and because they are all Americans and in that exuberant emotional state a winning team exudes, I hold my peace and listen, but take surreptitious notes.

"Your President – Prime Minister – whatever, he's one smart cookie! You got to face it. You Canadians were on the wrong track before he took over. Drugged on welfare! Babied from cradle to the grave by lefty governments! Fed a lot of bullshit about narrow-minded nationalism! Mulroney's going to change all that and it'll be good for you. *He* knows Canadians and Americans *belong* in the same bed."

"Mulroney? Hey, I love that guy! First time my company sent me up here to straighten out some labour trouble at our mines that red-assed Trudeau was running things – right into the ground! But now, if we had our own guy sitting in Ottawa he couldn't do better than Mister Mulroney!''

"It's been the hell of a long time coming, but you Canadians have finally seen the light. One continent. One *market*. And, why not? One people. It's gotta be.''

They lose interest in me and the talk veers off to multimillion-dollar deals to channel Canadian energy, and fresh water, into the United States. I ring for another drink and when the flight attendant brings it, he leans down and mutters in my ear: "These sons of bitches act like they've just bought Canada. The Conservative bastards have sold us down the drain!''

"Not so,'' I tell him. "Judas is *giving* Canada to the Yanks – on a silver platter.''

Déjà-vu . . . déjà-vu!

But it isn't really fair to call Mulroney and *all* the members of his cabal Judas Iscariots, Benedict Arnolds, Quislings, or the like. Mulroney is an honest man – according to his lights. He is being true to himself – in his own way. *He* certainly doesn't view himself as a traitor to Canada. On the contrary, he sees himself as an American missionary leading us into the fold. Remember that he was born and brought up in Baie Comeau, a U.S. fiefdom in Quebec owned by Colonel Robert McCormick of *Chicago Tribune* fame. Admiring the Americans comes naturally to him, since it has always paid good dividends. When Colonel McCormick visited his northern pulp and paper kingdom on ceremonial occasions, little Brian would sing Irish songs for his liege lord's entertainment – and would be rewarded with U.S. silver dollars. Then, when he was grown up, he went out into the wider world and became president of the so-called Iron Ore Company of Canada, a branch plant of the Hanna Mining Corporation of Cleveland, Ohio. Hanna, as Allan Fotheringham has pointed out, supplied their Canadian-born satrap "with an executive jet and an apartment over Central Park in New York and lots of goodies.''

■■■■■■■■■■■■■■■■■■■■■■■■■■■■■■

It is hardly to be wondered at that, in his current role as Vice-President in charge of Northern Regions, Mulroney does his dedicated best to please his patrons to the south.

God bless America!

October 21, 2007. I have just arrived at Montreal's bleak and decrepit Mulroney International Airport (once prosaically called Mirabel) after a long sojourn in Scandinavia. A posse of immigration officers has sternly informed me that I can no longer enter Canada. My name is in the U.S. Immigration and Naturalization Service's "Lookout Book," where I am listed as a subversive undesirable.

Waiting in the deportee's cage for the departure of the next Scandinavian Airlines flight, I do not feel too badly at being excluded from the land of my birth. After all, it isn't exactly Shangri-La these days. In fact, the poor devils who haven't been able to flee elsewhere tend to refer to it as New Siberia. Even seen from the air on the approach to Montreal, the desolation is brutally apparent. There is no lively display of autumnal colours because all the trees fit for pulping have been cut; and whatever was rejected has been killed by air pollution, leaving only skeletal sticks to rot amongst the abandoned little villages along the St. Lawrence. Almost all of Canada's manufacturing and industrial capacity has either withered on the vine or been transplanted south to the sun belt by its new owners, taking with it the jobs of millions of Canadians, but sending back into Canada an ever-growing plume of deadly fumes and toxic fall-out as fair exchange.

Waiting in the grubby detention cell, I seem to hear a beautifully timbred voice from another time chanting a mellifluous election pledge: "My government's first concern will be to create jobs . . . jobs . . . jobs." Ah, well, he never actually said who'd *get* those jobs.

There isn't even much employment in Canada now as hewers of wood and haulers of water. Automated machinery does most of what is necessary, governed by elec-

256

■■■■■■■■■■■■■■■■■■■■■■■■■■■■■■■

tronic gizmos in the hands of high-tech American wizards who are willing to work in Canada for a year or two because of the fat "isolation bonuses" they receive.

Farming? It is to laugh – or weep. Most of the remaining arable land north of the border belongs to enormous U.S. agribusiness syndicates devoted to mining raw botanical materials, such as corn, for industrial use down south. It is said that a quarter-million acres of Canadian agricultural land are now being mined out every year – reduced to sterile wastes of grey mud in the wet seasons, and spreading dust bowls in dry times. North American food crops are now mostly restricted to the western U.S. states, where they are irrigated to a fare-thee-well by the giant canals diverting Canadian rivers to the thirsty south. Not much of that food gets shipped up to Canada any more. Canadians haven't the money to buy it, and the population keeps on shrinking anyway. But hundreds of thousands of Canadians *have* found work of a sort in the California and Arizona croplands as migrant farm labourers alongside their Mexican compères. Peons from the north!

Truth to tell, about the only employment left at home is caretaking at U.S. bases and mining complexes, or guiding wealthy southerners in their never-ending pursuit of animals and birds to shoot and fish to catch in the few surviving forests and unpolluted waters. Most young male Canadians have been drafted or, for want of anything else to do, have volunteered into the U.S. armed forces, there to become mercenaries in the endless, bloody revolts against the empire being waged more and more successfully by "client states" possessed of more guts, so it appears, than Canadians can claim. The empire is in heavy trouble all around its shrinking periphery, while at its centre the savage, if undeclared, civil war between the ever-wealthier "haves" and the increasingly impoverished "have nots" waxes more ferocious day by day.

"What possessed you Canadians," a Finnish friend

asked me recently, "to throw yourselves into the arms of the American Empire, *not* when it was in the ascendant, but when it was obviously in its decline?"

I decided there is no point in thinking about that. Instead, I solace myself with the thought that I am really rather lucky not to have to spend even a few autumnal days in Canada now that the half-empty and fast-decaying cities must exist on a beggar's ration of heat, water, and electricity, which is all they are permitted because of the massive demands of the states at the heart of the new continental union.

A glum Immigration guard, bringing me a cup of ersatz coffee and a prefabricated doughnut for my dinner, seems to share this thought.

"Jesus, buddy, you don't know how lucky you are to be goin' back wherever you come from. Canada is for the fuckin' boids!"

There can be no other real choice open to a Canadian except to resist the Yanks and all their works so that we, as a people and a nation, may escape being ingested into the Eagle's gut, never to emerge again except as a patch of excrement upon the pages of world history . . .

Déjà-vu?

■■■■■■■■■■■■■■■■■■■■■■■■■■■■■■■■■
Acknowledgements

Margaret Atwood: A version of this article appeared in *The Globe and Mail* on November 5, 1987. It is excerpted from a speech given to the Parliamentary Committee on Free Trade.

Pierre Berton: A version of this article appears in *Why We Act Like Canadians*, published by McClelland and Stewart and Penguin of Canada Limited in 1987.

Allan Fotheringham: Another version of this article appeared in *Maclean's*.

Dr. David Suzuki: A version of this article appeared in *The Globe and Mail* on November 14, 1987.

Marjorie Cohen: A version of this article appeared in *The Globe and Mail* on October 12, 1987.

Mel Hurtig: From a presentation to the House of Commons Committee on External Affairs and International Trade, November 17, 1987.

Rick Salutin: A version of this article appeared in *The Globe and Mail* on November 5, 1987.

A.J.M. Smith: ''The Lonely Land'' is reprinted from *Poets Between the Wars*, edited by Milton Wilson, published by McClelland and Stewart, 1967.

We gratefully acknowledge the use of editorial cartoons from the following:

Aislin (Terry Mosher), *Montreal Gazette*
Bado (Guy Badeaux), *Le Droit d'Ottawa*
Josh Beutel, Saint John Telegraph-Journal
Sue Dewar, Calgary Sun
Frank Edwards, Kingston Whig-Standard
Bob Krieger, The Province, Vancouver
Roland Pier, Le Journal de Montréal
Dennis Pritchard, Saskatoon Star-Phoenix
Adriane Raeside, The Times-Colonist, Victoria